# RED
## LAND
### BLUE
#### LAND

# Claudio Hils

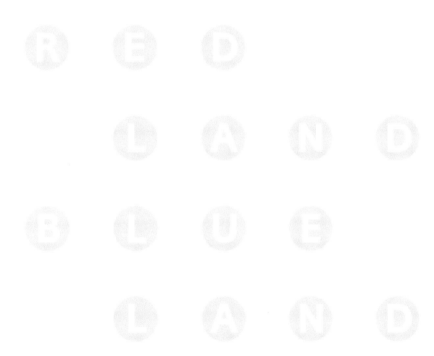

R E D

L A N D

B L U E

L A N D

Textbeiträge von | Accompanying essays by

Rolf Schönlau

Anna M. Eifert-Körnig

Hatje Cantz Verlag

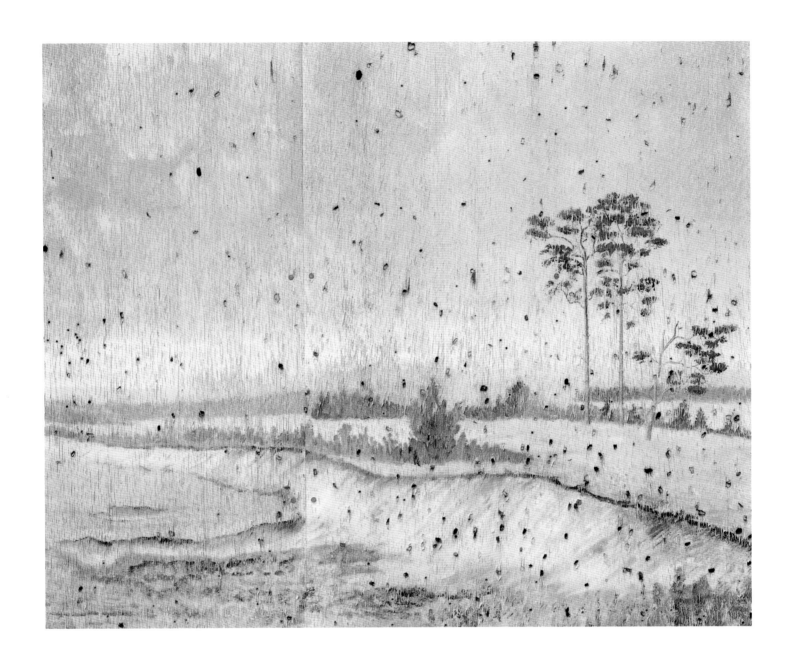

Gemalte Idealansicht der Senne
als Hintergrund der Kleinkaliberschießbahn Büren

Painted idealistic view of the Senne
as backdrop to the Büren Small Bore Range

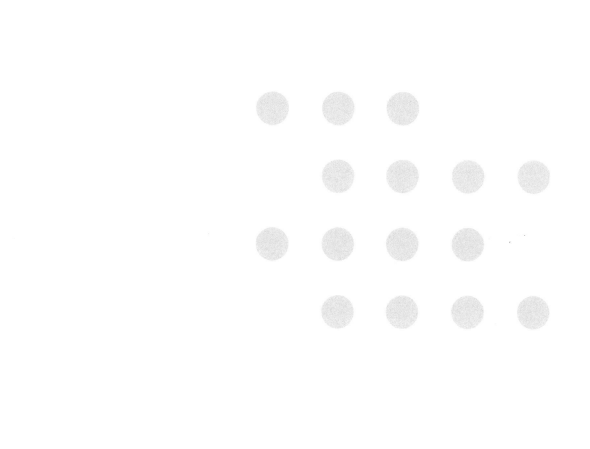

Inhalt | Contents

# Vorwort

## Foreword

*Red Land – Blue Land* heißt es in der Manöversprache, wenn ein Gelände zu Übungszwecken in Feindesland und Freundesland aufgeteilt wird. Wie etwa der Truppenübungsplatz Senne, STC (Sennelager Training Center) im Sprachgebrauch der britischen Streitkräfte, denen das Gebiet 1955 vertraglich zur Nutzung überlassen wurde. Von der ursprünglichen Sennelandschaft, die auf den Karten des 17. Jahrhunderts noch als *desertum sinedi*, also als Wüste, bezeichnet wird, hat nur der militärisch genutzte Teil etwas von seinem spezifischen Charakter bewahrt. Der Rest der ehemals 40 km langen und 3–15 km breiten Sandfläche mit dünenartigen Hügelreihen am Westrand des Teutoburger Waldes ist kaum noch als einheitlicher Landschaftsraum erkennbar.

Am 1.1.1001 bekam der Bischof von Paderborn die Senne von Kaiser Otto III. verliehen. Kein sehr wertvolles Lehen, denn die aus land- und forstwirtschaftlicher Sicht geringwertigen Böden waren allenfalls als Weideland geeignet. So behielt das Gebiet über viele Jahrhunderte den Charakter eines Niemandslandes, das sich unbeachtet durch die Territorien verschiedener westfälischer Herrschaften zog. Nur den Reisenden dürfte die Senne schon seit jeher ein Begriff gewesen sein, verliefen doch wichtige Fernstraßen durch die öde Sandheide. Dorfgründungen und später die Naturbegeisterung der Romantik trugen dazu bei, daß die Senne gegen Ende des 19. Jahrhunderts ihren abschreckenden Ruf verloren hatte. Etwa zur gleichen Zeit begann das Militär Interesse an dem Gebiet zu bekunden, das nach und nach aufgekauft wurde, bis 1939 die letzten Bewohner umgesiedelt waren. Aus dem ehemaligen Niemandsland war ein militärisches Sperrgebiet geworden.

Wie eine Enklave in bewohntem Gebiet erscheint der Truppenübungsplatz Senne, dessen Durchgangsstraßen zeitweise für den Transit geöffnet sind. Man fährt durch eine Landschaft, die aufs eigentümlichste mit militärischen Zeichen und Spuren durchsetzt ist. Ein Versuchsfeld des Krieges, auf dem die großen militärischen Auseinandersetzungen des Jahrhunderts ihren Niederschlag gefunden haben. Kriegsschauplätze aus allen Weltgegenden sind in der Senne versammelt: ein flutbarer Nachbau des Wolgabettes für Panzer-Tauchfahrten; ein Betonschiff zur Simulation der Anlandung in Korea; Schützengräben, wie sie die irakische Armee im Golfkrieg anlegte oder eine Dorfattrappe für den Orts- und Häuserkampf in Nordirland und anderswo.

Wenn auf einem Gelände wie dem Truppenübungsplatz Senne Bebauung und Besiedlung ebenso zur Disposition stehen wie Bewuchs und Gestalt des Bodens, erscheint das Verhältnis von Mensch, Natur und Technik auf dramatische Weise zugespitzt. Doch gerade in dieser instrumentalisierten Landschaft finden viele Tier- und Pflanzenarten, die auf der roten Liste stehen, noch ihre spezifischen Lebensräume vor. Ein Umstand, der zweifellos darauf zurückzuführen ist, daß es sich um ein weitgehend für die Öffentlichkeit gesperrtes Gebiet handelt.

Rolf Schönlau

8

*Red Land – Blue Land*: In the language of military manoeuvres, this refers to a piece of terrain divided into enemy territory and friendly territory for the purposes of combat exercises. An example of such terrain is the Senne, in the language of the British Armed Forces STC (Sennelager Training Centre). In 1955 the area was given to the British under contract for their exclusive use. Of the original Senne landscape which on the maps of the 17th century is characterized as *desertum sinedi* – or desert – only that section still used by the military has retained something of its specific character. The rest of the formerly 40 km long and 3–15 km wide surface of sand with dune-like hillocks on the western edge of the Teutoburger Forest, is now hardly recognisable as an integral landscape.

On 1.1.1001, King Otto III. gave the Senne to the bishop of Paderborn. The feif, however, was of precious little value since for the purposes of agriculture and forestry the soil was of little worth and was best suited as grazing land. In this way, the area retained its character as a no-man's-land over many centuries, extending unnoticed through the territories of various Westphalian rulers. The Senne has been known mainly to travellers, as major roads run through the desolate sandy moorland. The establishment of villages and later the romantics' enthusiasm for nature all contributed to the Senne finally losing its bad name by the close of the 19th century. At approximately the same time, the military authorities became interested in the area which they then gradually bought until, by 1939, the last inhabitants were finally relocated elsewhere. The former no-man's-land became a military prohibited zone.

The army training grounds at the Senne is like an enclave in an inhabited area, the through roads of which are periodically opened to transit. One drives through a landscape strangely interspersed with signs of the military: An experimental field of war upon which the greatest confrontations of this century have left their mark. War scenes from all areas of the world are enacted at the Senne: A reconstruction of the Volga Basin which can be flooded for amphibian tank manoeuvres, a concrete ship for practising a landing in Korea, trenches such as those constructed by the Iraqi army in the Gulf war or a reconstructed village for urban and house-to-house combat in Northern Ireland and elsewhere.

Where, on a terrain such as the Senne troop manoeuvres area, development and construction are at one's disposal as well as the growth and formation of the soil, the relationship between the human being, nature and technology would appear to have been radically intensified. Yet, it is precisely in this instrumentalized landscape that many threatened animal and plant species are still able to find their habitats. This circumstance doubtless results from the fact that the area is mostly prohibited to the public.

Rolf Schönlau

Rolf Schönlau

## Vom Niemandsland zum Sperrgebiet

## From No-Man's Land to Forbidden Zone

In den fünfziger Jahren in einer Sennerand-
gemeinde aufzuwachsen, dazu noch an einer Zufahrts-
straße zum Truppenübungsplatz – T-r-a-i-n-i-n-g A-r-e-a,
wie das Kind die englischen Wörter zu entziffern ver-
suchte –, das bedeutete, mitten in der Nacht durch vor-
beiratternde Panzer aus dem Schlaf gerissen zu werden.
Beim Frühstück hieß es dann: Wie im Krieg! Oder vielleicht: Wie damals in Haustenbeck! Damit konnte das
Kind etwas anfangen. Haustenbeck, das waren zer-
schossene Ruinen, ein zerfallener Feuerwehrturm, eine
kaputte Kirche, ein Friedhof und ein Aussichtsturm für
die Manöverbeobachter mit ihren rot- und blauschraf-
fierten Karten. Red Land – Blue Land: Rot für Feindesland, blau für Freundesland.

Im Herbst 1938, als die ersten Haustenbecker
schon umgesiedelt waren, fuhren ganze Panzer-
regimenter durch das Dorf, wußte die Mutter zu erzählen,
einmal eine motorisierte Kolonne von 35 km Länge. Das
war in dem Jahr, als das Aussaatverbot erlassen wurde,
mochte die Großmutter hinzugefügt haben. Es muß ein
ehemaliger Haustenbecker gewesen sein, der nicht müde
wurde zu erzählen, wie die Umsiedlung im einzelnen vor
sich ging. Obwohl noch viele Häuser bewohnt waren,
stellte das Militär im Juni 1939 neben dem Ortsschild

eine Tafel auf: „Lagerplatz Haustenbeck". Das Pfarrhaus
wurde zur Ortskommandantur, das Doktorhaus zur
Offizierswohnung, das Konsumgebäude zum Kranken-
revier, die Gastwirtschaft zum Offizierskasino und der
Saal zur Kantine.

Mit der Angst vor einer Umsiedlung hatten die
Haustenbecker seit 1890 gelebt, als das Kriegs-
ministerium damit begonnen hatte, insgeheim Land
anzukaufen. Selbst der zuständige Landrat war nicht
von Anfang an über den geplanten Militärübungsplatz
informiert gewesen. Bereits 1892 wurden die ersten
Truppen in Sennelager stationiert; zuerst bezogen sie in
Zelten Quartier, die im Krieg gegen Frankreich erbeutet
worden waren. Gleich im folgenden Jahr wurde der
Haustenbecker Ortsteil Taubenteich aufgekauft, so daß
der Übungsplatz von Westen her schon bis fast an das
Dorf heranreichte. Als 1935 mit Augustdorf ein zweiter
Sennestandort gegründet wurde, rief das die alten
Befürchtungen der Haustenbecker wach. Zu Recht, wie
sich zeigte, denn schon Anfang 1937 war der Übungs-
platz auch im Osten bis an die Dorfgrenzen vorgerückt.
Das Dorf war im Westen und Osten abgeriegelt und nur
noch über zwei Straßen mit der Außenwelt verbunden.
„Der polnische Korridor," so hieß es damals halb spöt-
tisch, halb betroffen, wenn die Rede auf Haustenbeck
kam.

Auf die Frage, was das zu bedeuten habe, bekam
das Kind nur zur Antwort, das sei einmal gewesen,
davon verstehe es noch nichts. Doch daß die Bewohner
Haustenbecks 1937 Passierscheine bekommen hatten,
die anfangs noch für den ganzen Platz galten, dann
nur für die Durchgangswege und schließlich allein für
den Weg zur Arbeit, darunter konnte sich das Kind
etwas vorstellen. Die Lastwagenfahrer, die mehrmals
täglich am Haus vorbeifuhren, um den feinen
Sennesand aus der Sandgrube zu holen, hatten so eine
Sondergenehmigung. Die Schäfer und die Förster hatten eine und die Schrankenwärter auch, die am

In the early 50's the child grew up in a village on the edge of the Senne, the military Senne with an access road to the T-r-a-i-n-i-n-g A-r-e-a. Deciphering the letters of the alphabet formed into unfamiliar words in the English language confused the child. They had a meaning: To be torn away in the depth of night from the folds of slumber by the sound of tanks rattling and tracks squealing past the house. At breakfast one would often hear the comment "Just like the War!" or perhaps "Like that time in Haustenbeck!". This was a place to which the child could relate. Haustenbeck. Haustenbeck was a bullet-riddled ruins, a wasted firehouse tower, a broken church and an abandoned cemetery; an observation tower for soldiers, standing vigil with their red- and blue-shaded maps, Red Land, Blue Land – a war game. Red for the enemy, and blue for friend.

As mother knew to tell, it was in the Autunm of 1938 – when the first Haustenbeckers were relocated – that whole Regiments of Armoured columns would drive through the village. Once, a motorised convoy more than 35 kilometres long passed through. That was the year seed planting was forbidden, grandmother added. It must have been a former Haustenbecker who never tired of relating in detail the story of how the resettlement progressed. In June 1939, even though many houses were still being lived in, the military authorities erected a board next to the village name: "Lagerplatz Haustenbeck". The priest's home became the village command centre, the doctor's house – officers' billets, the village shop – the sick bay, the inn – an officers' mess and the village hall – a soldiers' canteen.

Ever since the Prussian War Ministry had secretly begun to acquire land, the Haustenbeck villagers had been living in fear of compulsory purchase and resettlement. Even the relevant ministry had been unaware of the plans for turning the location into a military training area. However, by 1892 the first troops began to be stationed in Sennelager. At first they were quartered in bell tents, the spoils of the war against France. In 1893 Taubenteich, situated in the west side of the village, was purchased, so that the training area was already at that time approaching Haustenbeck's doorstep. The old fears were to re-surface in 1935, as Augustdorf acquired the status of a second Senne Garrison. These fears were confirmed in 1937 as the training area extended its boundaries, this time from the east side. Closed in from east and west, there were now only two inroads to the village. At that time, half in jest, when talk of Haustenbeck circulated, its location was referred to as the "Polish Corridor".

When the child asked what this meant, the only answer he received was, "at one time this was the case". Clearly, he was unable to comprehend the significance of this reply. However, that the residents of Haustenbeck held special passes, valid initially for the whole area, later limited to transit routes, and finally, only for the journey to work, was something to which he could relate. The truck driver who drove past the house many times a day hauling the fine Senne sand from the sandpit possessed a special permit. The shepherds, foresters and the guard also had one: He, who sat indolently beside the candy-striped barrier pole and who raised and lowered the red flag when the shooting commenced. Every child in the village was able to distinguish the sound of shooting from thunder. The explosions would rattle the window frames. It was said that on the periphery of the training area, windows were set more loosely in their frames than anywhere else: too firmly lodged and they would shatter.

For civilians, leaving the transit routes was strictly forbidden. "Blinds" (duds) was the word

11

Schlagbaum saßen und beim Schießen die rote Fahne hochzogen. Jedes Kind im Dorf wußte zwischen Donnern und Schießen zu unterscheiden. Das Knallen ließ die Fensterscheiben erzittern, die – so sagte man – im Sennerandgebiet lockerer als anderswo eingesetzt werden müßten, weil sie sonst platzen könnten.

Für Zivilpersonen war das Verlassen der Durchgangsstraßen strengstens verboten. Blindgänger, so hieß das Schreckenswort, das allen Kindern eingeimpft wurde. Doch zweimal im Jahr wurde das Verbot übertreten. Im Juli schlichen sich ganze Familien mit Milchkannen bewaffnet ins Sperrgebiet, weil dort die besten Heidelbeeren wuchsen. Und in klaren Novembernächten fuhr man in die Senne, um die Hirsche röhren zu hören. Im großen und ganzen hielt man sich jedoch an das Verbot. Selbst als der Großvater dem Kind das Stück Heide zeigte, das der Familie früher einmal gehört hatte, blieben sie auf der Straße.

Der Großvater hatte dort noch Ziegen gehütet. Die Senne ist ein uraltes Weideland, erklärte er dem Kind. Weide ist die ursprüngliche Bedeutung des Wortes *sinedi*, das sich über Sende zu Senne verwandelte. Das mochte er im „Gemeindeboten" gelesen haben. Bis Mitte des 17. Jahrhunderts trieben die Hirten aus den umliegenden Ortschaften ihr Vieh aus, ohne auf irgendwelche Grenzen zu achten. Als dann nach Ende des Dreißigjährigen Krieges die ersten Siedler in die Senne zogen, kam es zu Streitigkeiten, woraufhin die Nutzungsrechte zwischen den Dörfern festgelegt wurden. Die zweite Siedlungswelle nach dem Siebenjährigen Krieg brachte neue Streitigkeiten mit sich. Diesmal ging es insbesondere um das Recht, Plaggen zu stechen. Die Sennebauern, die kaum Getreide anbauen konnten, benutzten Heideplaggen als Streu für das Vieh und zur Ackerdüngung. Allein das Dorf Haustenbeck, das um 1800 auf etwa 100 Wohnstätten angewachsen war, benötigte 10.000 Fuder Plaggen und 5.000 Fuder Heide im Jahr.

Die Streitigkeiten zwischen den Sennedörfern wurden oft nachts ausgetragen. Man stahl sich gegenseitig die fertig gestochenen Plaggen oder brach in die Herde ein und nahm das Vieh mit. Um die eigenen Leute zu alarmieren, hatten die Haustenbecker, deren Höfe auf Rufweite verstreut lagen, eine besondere Methode entwickelt. Wer den Einbruch als erster bemerkte, schlug mit der Axt ein vereinbartes Signal gegen das Dielentor und rief zu seinen Nachbarn hinüber: „De Biursproke geut rund! – Olle Mann no Poppen Hobe – met scharpen Geschirr!" Das brauchte der Großvater nicht zu übersetzen, er sprach sowieso meist Plattdeutsch mit dem Kind.

Ob es auch der Großvater gewesen war, der von den „Plaggenwölfen" erzählt hatte? Oder eher der Lehrer im Heimatkundeunterricht? Jedenfalls stellte sich das Kind wilde Bestien darunter vor, die einem auflauerten, wenn man unerlaubterweise die Senne betrat. Da konnte die Mutter noch so oft beteuern, daß es die „Plaggenwölfe" schon lange nicht mehr gab. Für das Kind hausten sie in den Ruinen. Zur Beruhigung half dann nur das Bild, schmal und sehr lang, das über dem Ehebett der Großeltern hing: Die ewig blühende Heide mit dem Heiland und den Schäfchen.

Die wirklichen „Plaggenwölfe" waren Sennebauern, die Plaggen stachen, ohne darauf zu achten, daß die Heide nachwachsen konnte. Doch der Raubbau rächte sich. Mitte des 19. Jahrhunderts lag an vielen Stellen der Sand an der Oberfläche und wurde mit jedem Windstoß wie Meeresdünen weitergetrieben. Der Flugsand bedeckte oft ganze Äcker und vernichtete die Ernte. Im Winter stand das Schneewasser manchmal bis an die Fenster, weil es nicht abfließen konnte. Die jahrhundertealte genossenschaftliche Dorfverfassung, die auf gemeinsamer Benutzung der Senne gründete, erwies sich als nicht mehr praktikabel. Um die Eigenverantwortung der Bauern zu stärken, wurde jedem eine Parzelle zugewiesen, auf der er Heide schneiden und Plaggen stechen konnte.

drilled into the children and which was the source of most of their fears. Yet, twice a year the prohibition would be ignored. In July, whole families loaded with milk cans would slip into the closed area, as it was here that the best blueberries could be gathered. On clear November nights one drove into the Senne to hear the rutting stags. Generally, everyone respected the law and, even when grandfather showed the child the plot of heathland which once belonged to the family, they remained on the road.

Grandfather once had herded goats on this land. The Senne is ancient pasture land, he told the child. Pasture is the original meaning of the word "sinedi", which over the years became Sende and later Senne. Grandfather had remembered reading about it in the parish news. Until the middle of the 17th century, the herdsmen from the nearby villages and parishes had grazed their animals without having to pay heed to the question of boundaries. After the Thirty Years War, the first settlers moved into the Senne and it was at this time that confrontations began to erupt. The result was a division of the land for the seperate and individual use of the surrounding communities. The second wave of settlers came after the Seven Years War and were to be the cause of further confrontation. Now it became a question of turf-cutting rights. The Senne farmers, who were hardly able to harvest grain, used heather sod as litter for their animals and, after having been put to such use, it was then distributed on the fields as manure. In 1800, the village of Haustenbeck had 100 dwellings and needed 10,000 loads of rough cut heather sod and 5,000 loads of heather clippings for household bedding.

The rivalries and arguments between the Senne villages would often be conducted at night. There was theft of freshly cut turf and animals were stolen from the herds. In Haustenbeck, where all the farmyards were situated within shouting distance of each other, there developed a sort of oral telegraphic system: Whoever first noticed an incident of theft would bang a pre-established signal on his door post and would call across to his neighbour: "The farmer's message does the round. Everyone meet at Poppe's farm – and bring sharp knives!" Although grandfather spoke the message in Low German, there was no need to translate it, for he and the child used the dialect daily.

Whether it was grandfather who told of the "heather wolf" or the teacher during local history lessons, the child imagined that wild beasts would lurk in the shadows just wating to seize anyone who wandered into the Senne without permission. How often had mother regretted the fact that the heather wolf was no longer around. For the child, the beast lived in the shadows of every ruin. Only the picture above the grandparents bed, which depicted the everblooming heather, the Saviour and the browsing lambs, would soothe him.

The real "heather wolves" were the Senne farmers, who cut turf in the heath without ever caring if the heather would grow again. Yet, nature was to avenge herself. By the middle of the 19th century, large bare patches of fine white sand were visible. Each gust of wind blew up dried humus and fine grains. The flying sand often covered whole fields – spoiling pastures and crops. Sometimes, in winter, the melted snow could not drain away and the houses stood to their window sills in water. The old traditional farmers' arrangement which had held for hundreds of years was forgotten. To increase individual awareness and responsibility, each farmer was given a designated parcel of land where he could cut his heather or dig his turf.

Außerdem begann man damit, die freiliegenden Sandhügel mit Kiefern zu bepflanzen, der einzigen Baumart, die auf den nährstoffarmen Böden gut gedieh. Damit veränderte die Senne ihr Gesicht, und die seit Menschengedenken charakteristische Weitläufigkeit der Landschaft ging mehr und mehr verloren. Heute ist der Truppenübungsplatz Senne etwa zur Hälfte bewaldet. Neben der Kiefer als vorherrschender Baumart sind auch Fichten, Buchen, Eichen und Birken anzutreffen. Einzelstehende Eichen zeigen an, wo früher ein Haus stand. Birkenwäldchen deuten darauf hin, daß das Gelände in der jüngeren Vergangenheit anderweitig genutzt wurde.

Bei einem Klassenausflug ins Detmolder Landesmuseum hatten die Kinder alte Gemälde von der Senne gesehen: weit und breit kein Baum, Sanddünen wie am Meer und überall dichte Heide. Noch 1797 verglich ein Reisender die Fahrt durch die Senne mit einer Seefahrt, und er rief erleichtert: „Land", als er am Ende der Sandheide endlich wieder Bäume entdeckte. Auch der Großvater wußte zu berichten, daß das Heidekraut in seiner Jugend viel üppiger gewesen war. Die ersten Siedler Mitte des 17. Jahrhunderts sollen es sogar in brusthohen Büschen vorgefunden haben, mit Stengeln dick wie Flaschenhälse. Die Heide lieferte ihnen Streu für das Vieh, Dünger, Heizmaterial und Nahrung für Schafe, Ziegen und Bienen. Wenn es in der Heide brannte, was im Sommer immer wieder passierte, verloren die Bauern ihre Lebensgrundlage. Deshalb war es den Schäfern seit dem großen Sennebrand von 1790 nur noch erlaubt, „aus einer wohlbekapselten Pfeife in der offenen Senne zu rauchen." Diese Geschichte wurde immer wieder beim Heidefest im August erzählt, wo das ganze Dorf, die Kinder voran, mit Musik in die Heide zog und die neue Heidekönigin kürte.

Das ganze Leben der Sennebauern drehte sich um die Heide, denn die Böden waren für viele andere Pflanzen schlecht geeignet. Der Grund dafür ist die Ortsteinschicht, eine verhärtete, schwärzlich-braune Sandschicht unter der Oberfläche, die sich aus herabgeschwemmtem Humus und ausgelaugten Eisenbestandteilen des Sandes gebildet hat und jeden weiteren Pflanzenwuchs hemmt. Wirklich kulturfähig ist der Senneboden erst, wenn die Ortsteinschicht gebrochen und an der Oberfläche verwittert ist. Dazu muß mehrere Spatenstiche tief gepflügt werden. Die armen Sennebauern hatten jedoch kaum Zugvieh, so daß es oft bei der Oberflächenbehandlung blieb und die anfangs guten Erträge schnell abnahmen.

Die Armut unter den Sennebauern war sprichwörtlich. Der durchschnittliche Nachlaß eines Haustenbeckers um 1720 betrug: 1 Kuh, 1 Bett, 1 Alltagskleid, 1 eisern Pott. Oder wenn es hoch kam: 1 Pferd, 1 Kuh, 1 Kessel von 3 Maß, 1 eisern Pott, 1 Bett, 1 Karre, 1 Alltagskleid. Einen Kupferkessel und ein Sonntagskleid zu besitzen, bedeutete schon einen seltenen Reichtum.

Die Einführung der Kartoffel Ende des 18. Jahrhunderts muß eine Erlösung von den davor regelmäßig wiederkehrenden Hungersnöten gewesen sein. Das erklärt die hohe Wertschätzung, die der Kartoffel im gesamten Sennegebiet zuteil wurde. Die Großmutter beklagte zwar immer wieder den trockenen Sandboden, doch für die Kartoffeln, sagte sie, sei er vorzüglich geeignet. Da die Bodenerträge trotzdem oft nicht ausreichten, um die Familie zu ernähren, hielten sich viele Sennebauern mit Spinnen und Weben über Wasser. Auch davon sprach die Großmutter oft und zeigte dann auf ihre Anrichte, die aus dem Eichenholz des alten Webstuhls gefertigt war. Außerdem gab es in den Sennedörfern viele Wanderarbeiter. Schon seit Mitte des 18. Jahrhunderts waren die Männer zum Torfstechen nach Holland gezogen. Später gingen sie als Ziegler ins Ruhrgebiet, nach Frankfurt und Brandenburg, ja sogar bis nach Schweden und Rußland.

A programme was initiated for planting Scots pines on the bare sandhills – the only species of tree capable of surviving the poorly nourished ground. As a consequence, the face of the Senne was to change. From time immemorial, the Senne had been characteristically a landscape through which one could walk for hours without seeing a tree. Today, more than half of the training area is forested. In addition to conifers, there are an increasing number of beech, birch and oak. Single oaks indicate the former site of a house. Birch copses indicate that land has been put to different uses in the more recent past.

During a school outing to the Detmold Landesmuseum, the child looked at old paintings of the Senne. Wherever one looked no trees were in sight. All the paintings depicted sand dunes, just like those one can see at the seaside, and in all directions thick heather. As far back as 1797, a traveller compared a journey through the Senne to a sea voyage. When completing his trip through the sandy heath he cried out, "Land-ho" and was relieved to see a tree again. Grandfather was able relate with certainty how in his youth the heath was much wilder. In the 17th century, the first settlers discovered bushes that were chest high with branches as thick as bottle necks. The plant provided litter for their animals, bedding for their households, manure for their fields, fuel for their fires and nourishment for their sheep, goats and bees. In the Summer, when the heath burned, as it often did, farmers would lose their livelihoods. Following the great Senne fire of 1790, shepherds were only permitted to smoke a "lidded pipe" in open areas of the Senne. This story was often repeated at heather festivals in August when the whole village, lead by children and musicians, went to the heath to choose the new Heather Queen.

The whole life of the Senne farming family revolved around heather, as the soil was too poor for almost any other plant. The primary reason for this was that it was comprised of a hardened, black-brown sand which formed itself from washed out humus and leached iron (podsol) which inhibited plant development, a feature indicative of a heathland. The Senne ground is only really capable of cultivation when this layer is broken and the top soil well weathered. To achieve this, many spade depths must be turned over. The inhabitants were the poorest of farmers and for this reason could afford practically no draught animals, so that usually only the upper layer of soil could be worked, and this soil gave only a mediocre yield.

The poverty among these farmers was proverbial. In 1720, the average Haustenbecker bequeathed: 1 cow, 1 bed, 1 working suit/dress, 1 iron pot. A very good inheritance comprised: 1 horse, 1 cow, 1 kettle with a 3 litre volume, an iron pot, 1 bed, a wheelbarrow, 1 set of working clothes. To own or be in possession of a copper kettle and Sunday clothes was a sign of rare wealth.

The introduction of the potato at the end of the 18th Century must have relieved the frequent hunger of the inhabitants. Throughout the Senne area potatoes were highly valued. Grandmother always condemned the dry sand soil but for the potato, she said, it was ideal. Often, however, a family could not feed itself on just one crop. In order to keep their heads above water, many spun wool or wove cloth. Grandmother often spoke of this and, when doing so, would show off her sideboard which had been built from the remains of an old weaving loom. Many people from the Senne villages left to find work. As early as the mid 19th century, men went to Holland to cut turf. Later, others went to the Ruhr region to make rooftiles or bricks, to Frankfurt and Brandenburg and even as far as Sweden and Russia.

15

Ihren abschreckenden Ruf einer menschenfeindlichen Ödnis verlor die Senne erst gegen Ende des 18. Jahrhunderts, als sich die empfindsamen Seelen der Romantik auch diesem Stück reiner urwüchsiger Natur nicht verschließen konnten. Gegen Ende des 19. Jahrhunderts dann fand die Senne in Hermann Löns einen ihrer glühendsten Verehrer. Vorbei an Quellsümpfen und mitten durch enkeltiefen Treibsand mußte er sich seinen Weg bahnen, um zu ihrem Geheimnis vorzudringen: „Und da sah ich sie auch, sah das gute Gesicht der ernsten, stillen Frau, und meine Augen nur grüßten sie, Frau Einsamkeit."

Die Soldaten der Alliierten Truppen, die 1991 in Sennelager auf den Wüstenkrieg am Golf vorbereitet wurden, dürften wohl kaum so gut auf den Sennesand zu sprechen gewesen sein. Genausowenig wie der Großvater, der 1914 dort den letzten Schliff bekommen hatte. Der Sennesand stammt aus der Eiszeit, hatten die Kinder im Heimatkundeunterricht gelernt. Als das Eis schmolz, das sich vor dem Teutoburger Wald staute, blieb der Sand zurück. Erst weit vom Gebirge brechen die unter dem Sand hinströmenden zahlreichen Quellen hervor. Sie haben viele Meter tiefe Bachtäler in den Boden gegraben, deren kräftige Vegetation in krassem Gegensatz zu den ausgedehnten Heide- und Trockenrasengebieten steht.

Das Dorf Haustenbeck verdankt seine Gründung einem dieser tief eingeschnittenen Bachtäler. Als Handel und Verkehr nach dem Dreißigjährigen Krieg wieder aufblühten, setzte der regierende Graf Hermann Adolf zur Lippe alles daran, den bestehenden Straßenverlauf durch sein Gebiet beizubehalten. Da das Haustenbachtal eine der größten Verkehrsbehinderungen darstellte, begann man 1659 mit dem Bau eines festen Damms, zu dessen Sicherung ein Dorf mit einem Wirtshaus für die reisenden Kaufleute gegründet wurde.

Im Landesmuseum gab es auch ein altes Kirchenfenster aus Haustenbeck zu sehen, mit dem Namen und Zeichen eines Bremer Kaufmanns. Das hatte der Lehrer bestimmt zum Anlaß genommen, um vom Frankfurter Weg und den anderen wichtigen Verkehrswegen zu erzählen, die seit dem Mittelalter durch die Senne führten. Ob er in diesem Zusammenhang auch Pfarrer Winand erwähnte, ist ungewiß. Wenn ja, dann hat er bestimmt das eine oder andere Detail weggelassen.

Haustenbeck bekam 1671 einen eigenen Pfarrer zugesprochen, den „abgestandenen Pastor" Joachim Winand aus Heiligenkirchen, der wegen Trunksucht seines Amtes enthoben worden war. Was noch fehlte, war eine Kirche. Als sie 1682 nach mehr als zehnjähriger Bauzeit endlich im Rohbau stand, war für weitere Arbeiten kein Geld mehr vorhanden. Pfarrer Winand kam nun auf die Idee, die verkehrsgünstige Lage seiner armen Gemeinde zu nutzen und die durchreisenden Kaufleute um Spenden für die Kirchenfenster zu bitten. Als Gegenleistung konnten die Geldgeber ihre Namen, Zeichen und Hauswappen in den Fenstern verewigen lassen. Insgesamt 39 Kaufleute von Basel bis Bremen nahmen die Gelegenheit wahr, den Durchreisenden ihre Handelshäuser zu präsentieren. 1685 fand die erste feierliche Sonntagspredigt in der neuen Kirche statt, womit die Wirtshauspredigten ein Ende hatten.

Bleibt noch von einem Geheimnis zu sprechen, der Panzerversuchsstation. So nannten alle im Dorf die kleine Fabrikhalle am Ortsausgang. Fotografieren verboten, stand auf einem Schild. Der Vater erzählte von einem Tüftler und Erfinder, der dort arbeitete und irgendwelche Verbesserungen an den Panzern vornahm. Das stimmte wohl auch, aber daß der Name von der ehemaligen Panzerversuchsstation Haustenbeck stammte, erfuhr das Kind erst viel später. Die Dorfbewohner hatten auch nichts davon gewußt, daß der legendäre Kampfpanzer Tiger ganz in ihrer Nähe entwickelt worden war. Als die Amerikaner im April 1945 die Senne

At about the beginning of the 18th century the Senne began to lose its terrifying reputation as a wasteland inimicable to habitation, as sensitive souls were unable to exclude this island of pure nature from their romanticism. Toward the end of the 19th century, the Senne found one of its most ardent admirers in the author Hermann Löns. Passing quagmired springs and forcing his way through ankle deep sand he advanced upon the innermost secret of the Senne: "And there I saw her too, saw the good and wistful countenance of a woman at rest, and my eyes could only greet her, Frau Solitude."

The soldiers of the Alliance Troups, who were at Sennelager in 1991 preparing for the Gulf War, probably had little good to say about the Senne Sand. No less so than grandfather who received his final polish here before marching off in 1914 to the First World War. The Senne sand had its birth during the Ice Ages, so the children learned in their local history lessons. As the ice, stacked up against the Teutoburger Ridge, began to melt, the sand remained. A short distance from the stone ridge, springs rose up through the sand. This constant flow of water gouged deep ravines and valleys in the thick sand bed, which support dense vegetation standing as if mocking the worn and poorly nourished thin grass on the surrounding sand.

The Haustenbeck settlement owes its existence to one of these deep stream valleys. As commerce and traffic re-asserted themselves following the Thirty Years' War, the ruling Duke, Hermann Adolf zur Lippe, did everything in his power to maintain the roads passing through his land. The Haustenbeck valley posed one of the greatest barriers to trade and traffic and, in 1659, work was started on an imposing dam. To ensure the safety of this edifice and to serve passing travellers, the village and an inn were established.

In the Detmold Landesmuseum an old church window from Haustenbeck is on display, showing the name and trademark of a businessman from Bremen. The teacher had taken pains to describe this and the importance of the Frankfurt route as a trade route which had passed through the Senne since the Middle Ages. Whether he spoke of Father Winand in the lesson is difficult to recall but if he did, he most likely left out the one or the other detail.

In 1671, the village of Haustenbeck was promised its own priest. The designated churchman was Joachim Winand from Heiligenkirchen, who had been de-frocked due to his predilection for drink. All that he needed in Haustenbeck was a church. In 1682, after more than 10 years building, the funding ran dry and all that had been achieved was the construction of an outer shell. Father Winand decided to raise subscriptions from travellers passing through his poor parish. He chose to look for donations by promising church windows, in which the donor could have his own name, trademark and arms preserved for posterity. Altogether, 39 business people from Basel to Bremen took up the offer, to make their business names known to other travelling merchants. The first Sunday sermon was heard in the new church in 1685, bringing an end to the services that had until then been held at the inn.

There now remains only one last secret to tell. The Tank Trials Establishment. This was the name everyone in the village gave to the little factory shed on the outskirts of the village. "Photography Forbidden" was written on a sign. Father spoke of an inventor and tinkerer who worked there and undertook alterations, adjustments, or improvements to tanks. This was true but the child was only to discover much later that the title referred to the Tank Trials Establishment of Haustenbeck. Even the villagers were unaware that the legendary Tiger battle

erreichten und die streng geheimgehaltene Versuchs-
station mit Tauchbecken entdeckten, ließen sie sich als
erstes zeigen, daß der Tiger tatsächlich in der Lage war,
bis zu 4,50 Meter tief zu tauchen.

Nach Kriegsende zogen Leute aus den umliegenden
Städten in die Senne und holten sich Fenster, Türen,
Dachziegel und andere Materialien, um ihre zerbombten
und beschädigten Häuser zu reparieren. Haustenbeck
stand schließlich erst wenige Jahre leer, und viele Häuser
waren noch intakt. Diese Plünderungen wurden allerdings schnell unterbunden von der britischen Besat-
zungsmacht, die den Platz kontrollierte. 1955 wurde der
Truppenübungsplatz den britischen Streitkräften vertraglich zur Nutzung überlassen. 1965 bekam das Kind
dann ein Bild davon, wie es in der verbotenen Senne
aussah. Das Fernsehen brachte Aufnahmen vom Truppenübungsplatz, als Königin Elisabeth II. die Truppen der
britischen Rheinarmee auf dem Paradeplatz an der
Windmühle inspizierte.

Von einem weiteren hohen Gast in der Senne muß
die Rede sein, von Raissa Gorbatschowa, der Frau des
sowjetischen Ministerpräsidenten, die 1989 den soge-
nannten Russenfriedhof besuchte. Russenfriedhof?
Nein, davon hatte das Kind nie etwas gehört. Auch
nichts vom Stalag 326, in dem die 65.000 vorwiegend
sowjetischen Kriegsgefangenen umkamen, die auf dem
Friedhof begraben sind. Wie hätte das Kind das auch
erfahren sollen, wo doch erst im Jahre 1996 in einem ehemaligen Arrestgebäude des Lagers eine Dokumentations-
stätte eingerichtet wurde?

Für das Kind gab es einen Ort in der Senne, der mit
besonderem Schrecken verbunden war: Staumühle, seit
1947 ein Lager für junge Strafgefangene. Ursprünglich
als Kriegsgefangenenlager des 1. Weltkriegs gegründet,
war Staumühle Mitte der 20er Jahre Ferienlager für
„licht- und lufthungrige Kinder aus den Mietskasernen
der Großstädte des Ruhrgebietes", wie es damals hieß.

Das mochte dem Kind erzählt worden sein, nicht jedoch,
daß Staumühle von 1945–47 ein Internierungslager gewesen war, wo auch die ehemaligen Naziführer des
Dorfes eingesessen hatten. Gleich 1933 hatte der
Freiwillige Arbeitsdienst in Staumühle Quartier bezogen,
um heimlich die Schießstände und Straßen in der Senne
auszubauen. Aus dieser Zeit stammte auch das soge-
nannte Russendorf, ein zu Übungszwecken original nach-
gebautes russisches Dorf mit Häusern, Ziehbrunnen und
allem, was dazugehört. Diese Dorfattrappe in der Nähe
von Haustenbeck wurde erst gegen Ende des Kalten
Krieges abgerissen.

Die Haustenbecker Ruinen dagegen stehen noch.
Die Panzer fahren schon lange nicht mehr durchs Dorf,
doch geschossen wird wie eh und je. Die Schrankenwärter sitzen immer noch in ihren grünen Häuschen und
ziehen beim Schießen die rote Fahne hoch. Auf dem
Gelände des Stalag befindet sich heute eine Polizei-
schule. Die Schäfer ziehen wie früher mit ihren Herden
durch die Senne und halten die Schießbahnen frei. Das
Heidelbeerpflücken ist aus der Mode gekommen, und
das Heidefest wird auch nicht mehr wie früher gefeiert.
Doch die Hirschbrunft lockt immer noch die Leute an.
Neuerdings gibt es einen Hermann-Löns-Wanderweg,
aber der führt am eigentlichen Sennegebiet vorbei. Zum
Betreten braucht man nach wie vor eine Sondergenehmigung. Ortskundige benutzen die Straßen durch
den Truppenübungsplatz auch heute noch gern als
schnellste Verbindung zwischen den umliegenden Ortschaften. Und wer über die Panzerstraße mit ihrem
blauen Basaltpflaster fährt, auf dem die Reifen so
unverwechselbar singen, erlebt die Senne aus der seit
Jahrhunderten vorherrschenden Sichtweise des Transit-
reisenden, dem heute bei Strafe verboten ist, was er
früher aus Angst vermied: von der Strecke abzuweichen.

tank had been developed near their village. When the Americans reached the Senne in 1945 and found the Trials Establishment and its diving dock, they wanted to see whether the Tiger really was built to dive and move at 4.5 metres underwater.

At the end of the war, strangers came to the Senne to fetch stone, roof tiles, windows and doors, bricks and timber, to repair their own houses which had been bombed. Haustenbeck had only been empty for a few years and most of the houses were still intact. The plundering was quickly stopped by the British Occupation Force, which had the training area under its control. In 1955, the Training Area was contractually put at the disposal of the British Forces. Queen Elizabeth II inspected the troops of the British Rhine Army in 1965 on the parade grounds at Winning Mill and it was through television coverage of the event that the child had an idea of what the forbidden Senne actually looked like.

A description ought to be given of another VIP guest at the Senne: Raissa Gorbatschowa, wife of the former Soviet Prime Minister who visited the so-called Russian Cemetery in 1989. Russian Cemetery? The child had never heard the term. Nor had he ever heard of 65,000 mostly Russian prisoners of war who died in Stalag 326 and who were now buried a short distance away. How could he have known this, seeing as it was not until 1996 that a documentation center was set up in a former arrest building on the site of the former camp?

For the child there was only one place in the Senne that was associated with a special fear. Staumühle. From 1947 on, it had become a type of borstal institution for young offenders. Originally, it had been set up for PoWs from the First World War. In the middle of the 1920's it was a holiday camp for youngsters otherwise deprived of "good light and

fresh air in the tenements of the large towns of the Ruhr". The child was told this. He had not been told that from 1945 – 1947 it had been an internment camp, where the former village NAZI leader had been held for de-nazification. In 1933, the Voluntary Works Service had taken up quarters in Staumühle, to quietly improve the ranges and roads in the Senne. During this time, the so – called Russian exercise village was built, replicating an actual village with houses and a well and all the necessary features. This village, close to the outskirts of Haustenbeck, was demolished toward the end of the Cold War.

The Haustenbeck ruins still stand. Tanks no longer drive through the village but, just as before, the firing continues. The guards sit, as always, in their little green painted houses and put up the red flags before firing. A police training school has been built on the grounds of Stalag 326 and, as in days gone by, the shepherds wend their way through the Senne, their flocks keeping the grass short on the firing ranges. Blueberry picking is out of fashion these days and the heather festival is no longer celebrated as it once was. Deer rutting attracts visitors as it always has. Most recently, a street has been named Hermann Löns Weg but it passes by the actual Senne. To access the training area one needs, as one always has, a special permit. Knowledgeable locals use the roads and ways through the Senne, as they always have, as the easiest and quickest connection to neighbouring parishes and communities. Yet, whoever should drive on the closed tank roads, with their blue cobblestones, upon which the wheels sing their unmistakable melody, he will view the Senne as commuters always have done for many hundreds of years, to whom it is forbidden on pain of penalty what was earlier avoided out of fear: to deviate from the road.

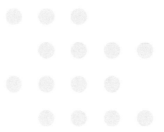

Blick vom Haustenbecker Turm:
1940/41 zur Artilleriebeobachtung
und Brandwache erbaut

View from the Haustenbeck Tower.
Built 1940/41 as an artillery observation
post and fire watch tower

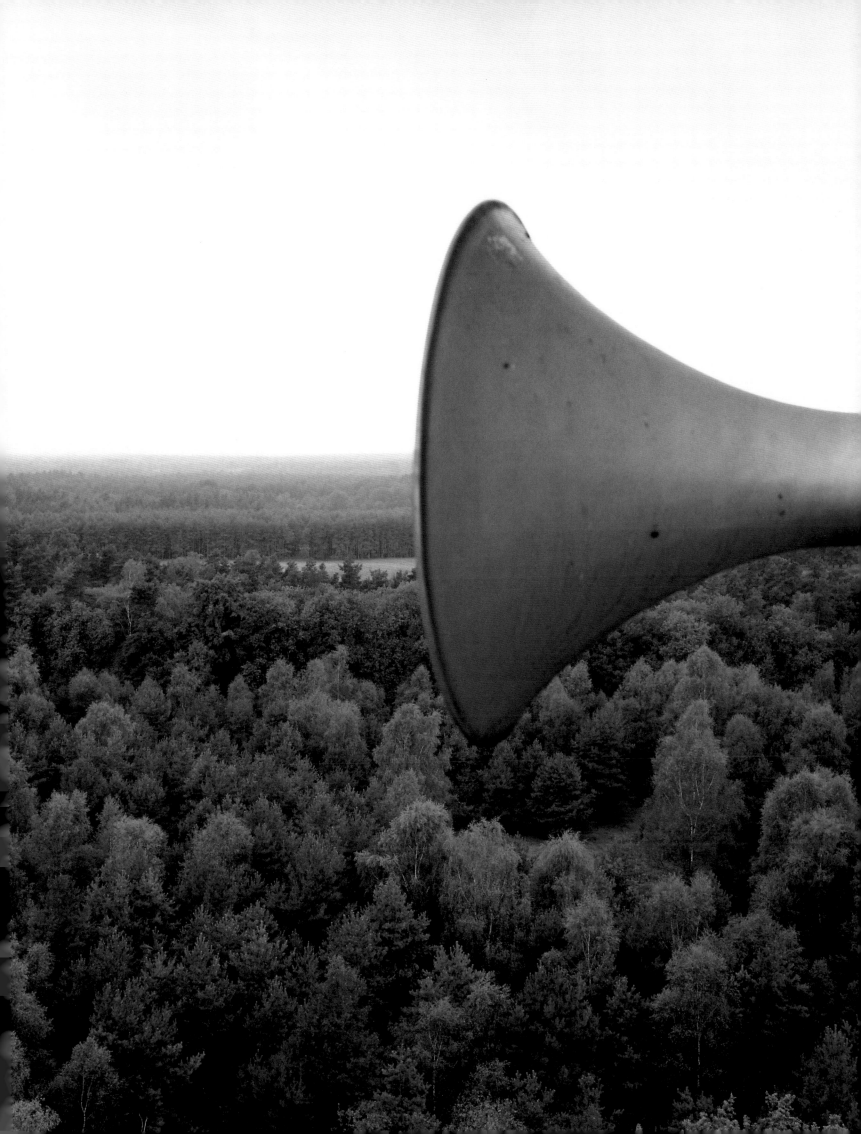

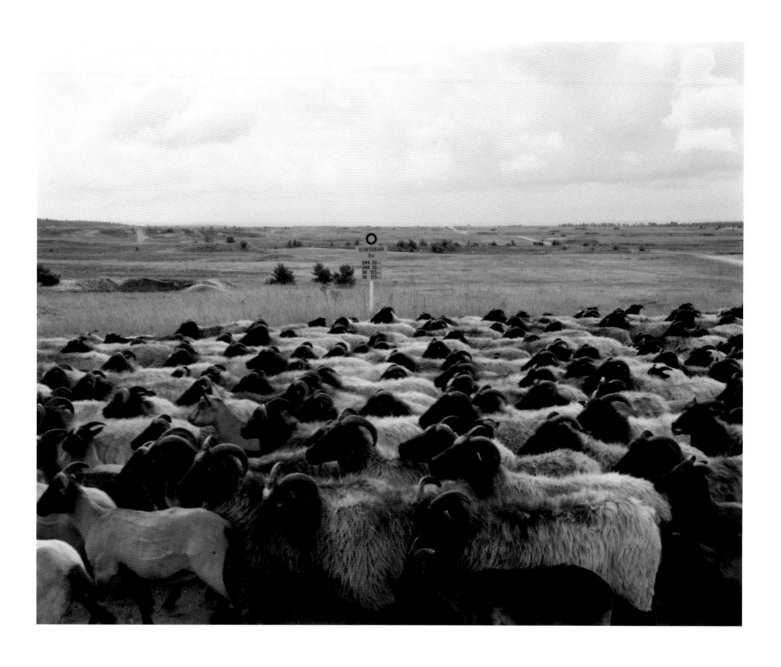

Bravo-Bahn mit Schafherde
zum Freihalten der Schießbahnen

Bravo Field Firing Area with flock of sheep
used for cropping the grass on firing areas

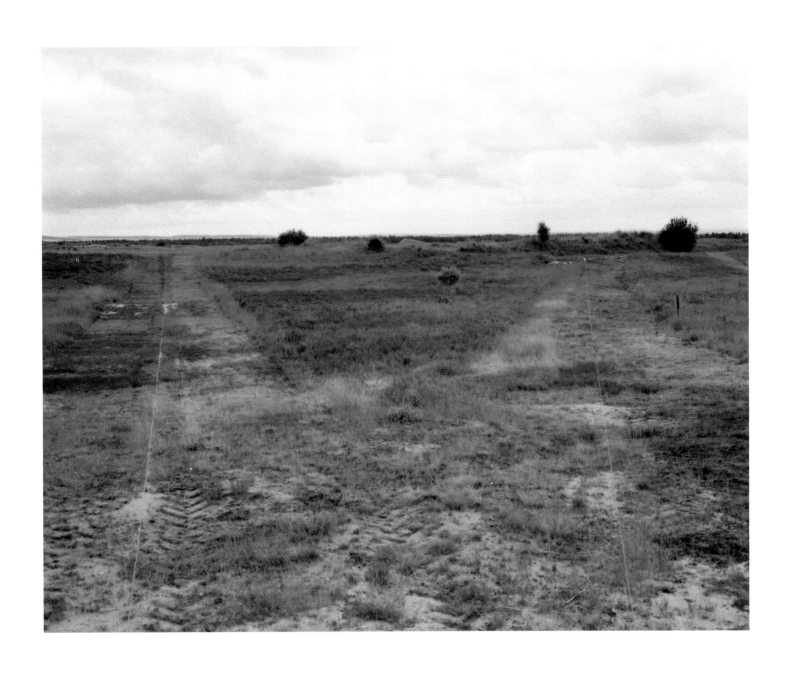

Lima-Bahn mit Seilzügen
für bewegliche Ziele

Lima Field Firing Area with cable runs
for moving targets

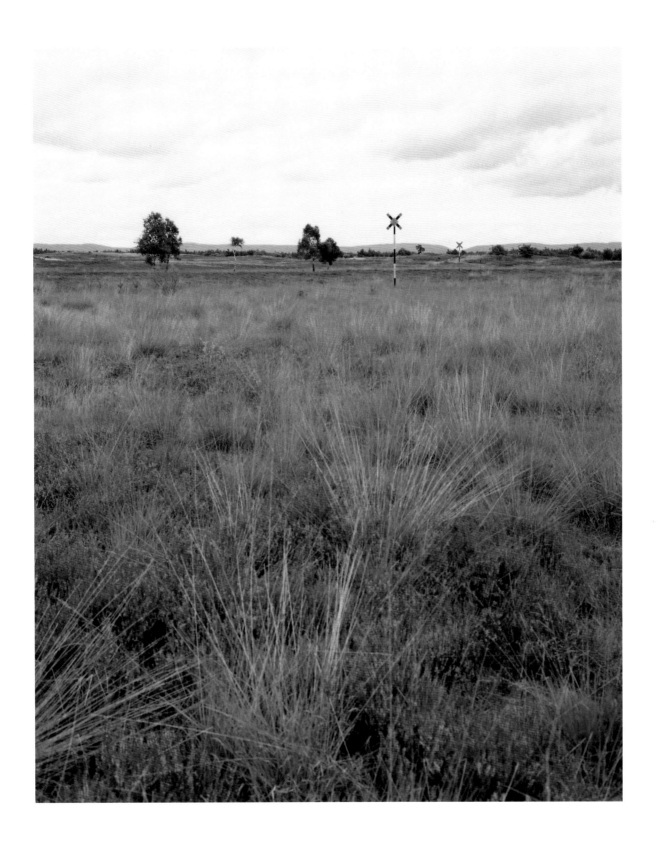

Golf-Bahn mit Schießbahnbegrenzungen | Golf Field Firing Area with boundary markers

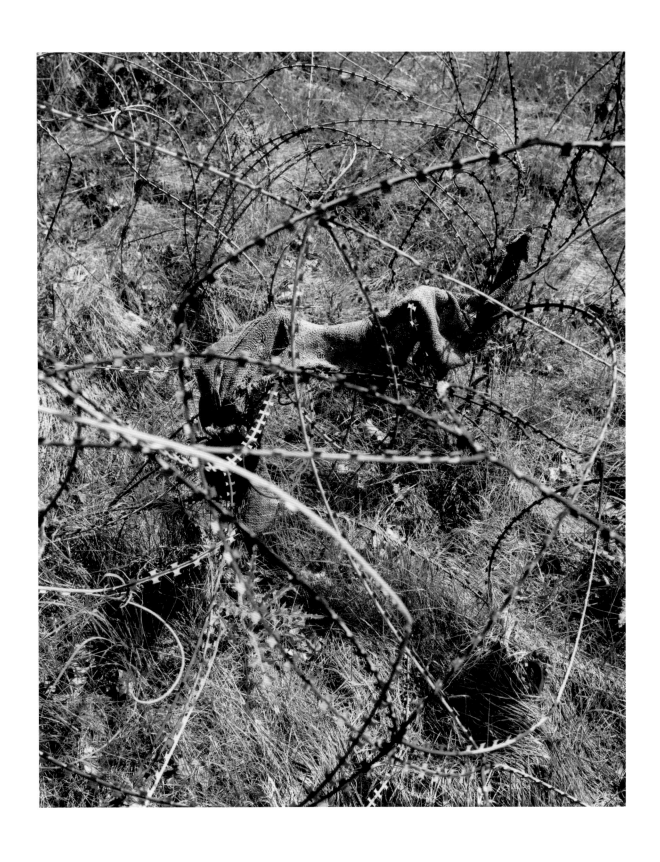

S-Draht auf der
Nachtkampfbahn Hannover

Barbed wire on
Hanover Night Movement Course

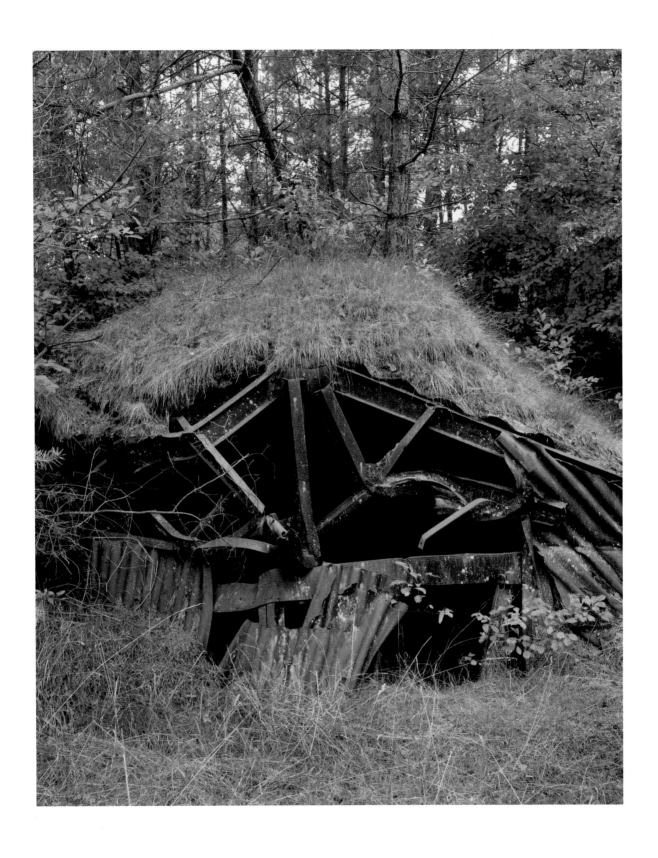

Pferdeunterstand aus der Zeit vor dem
1. Weltkrieg am Diebesturm

Cavalry stable under
Diebes Tower from WW I era

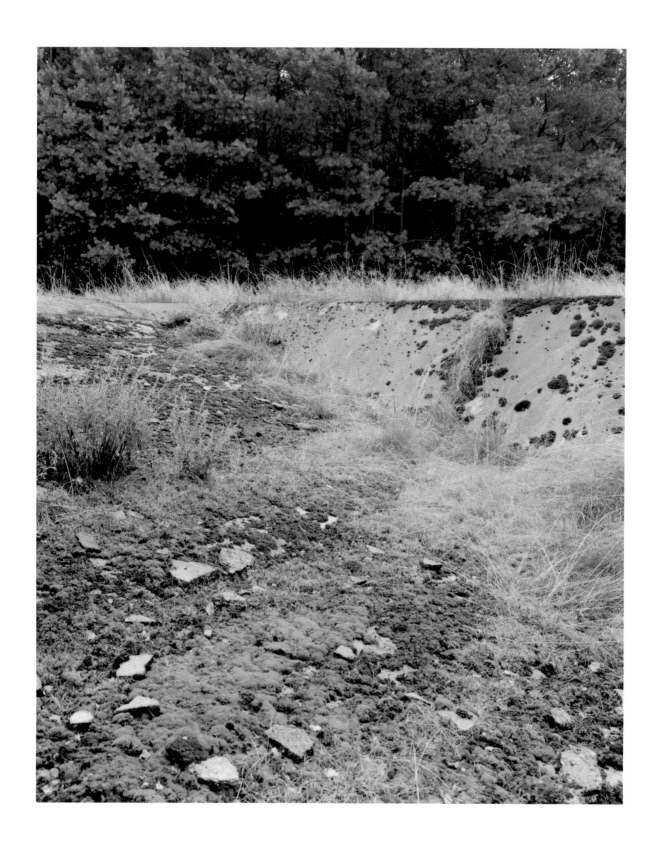

Flutbarer Nachbau des Wolgabettes
auf der Panzerversuchsstation Haustenbeck:
1938 für Panzer-Tauchfahrten erbaut,
1948 gesprengt

Replica of Volga river, floodable at
the Tank Trials Establishment, Haustenbeck.
Built in 1938 for tank snorkelling,
demolished in 1948

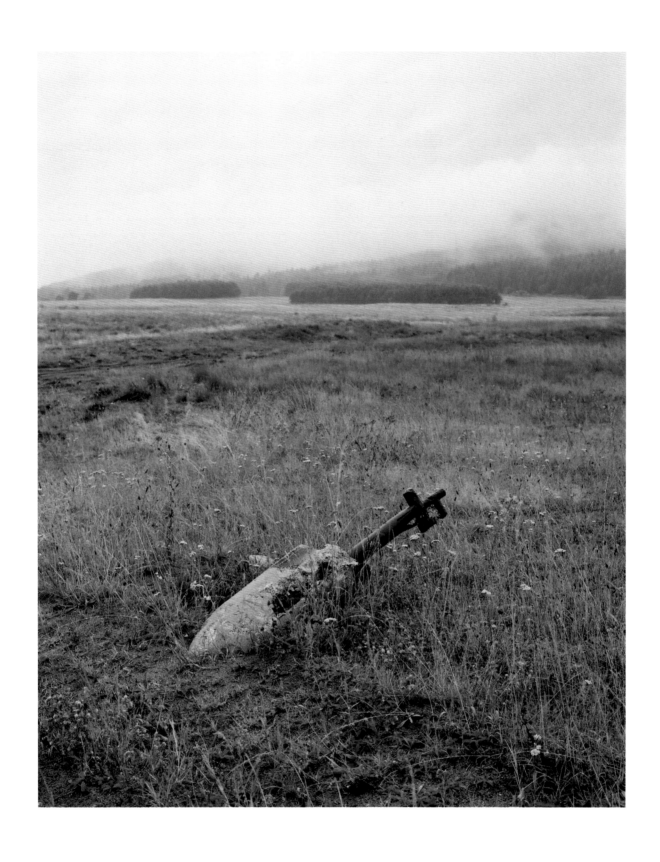

Schein-Flugplatz Stapel, benutzt von 1936 bis
1951 als Abwurfbahn für Bombenattrappen,
von 1939 bis 1945 zur Ablenkung
von alliierten Bombenflugzeugen

Decoy Airfield Stapel, used from
1936 to 1951 for practice bombing
and to attract allied bombs
between 1939 and 1945

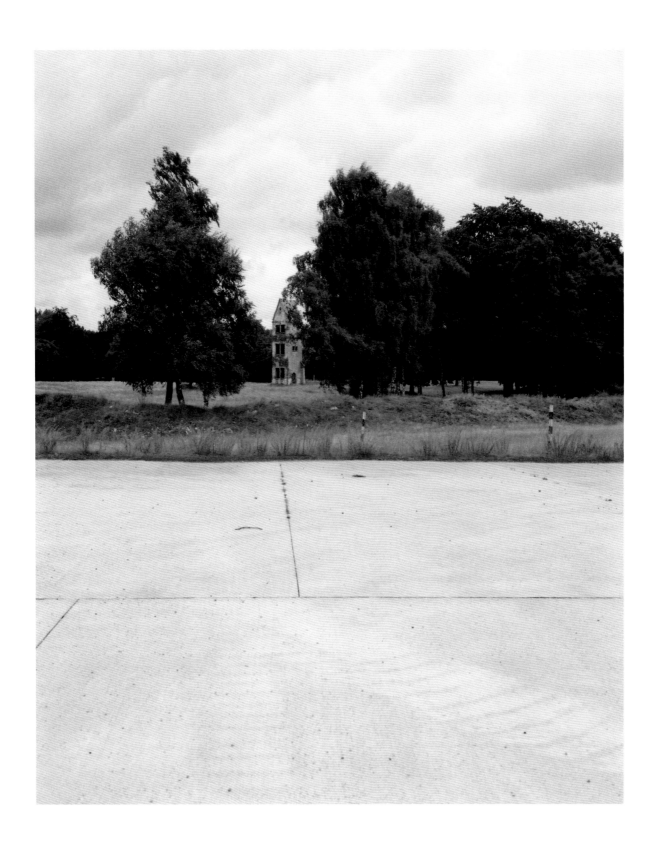

Haustenbecker Feuerwehrturm | Haustenbeck fire hose tower

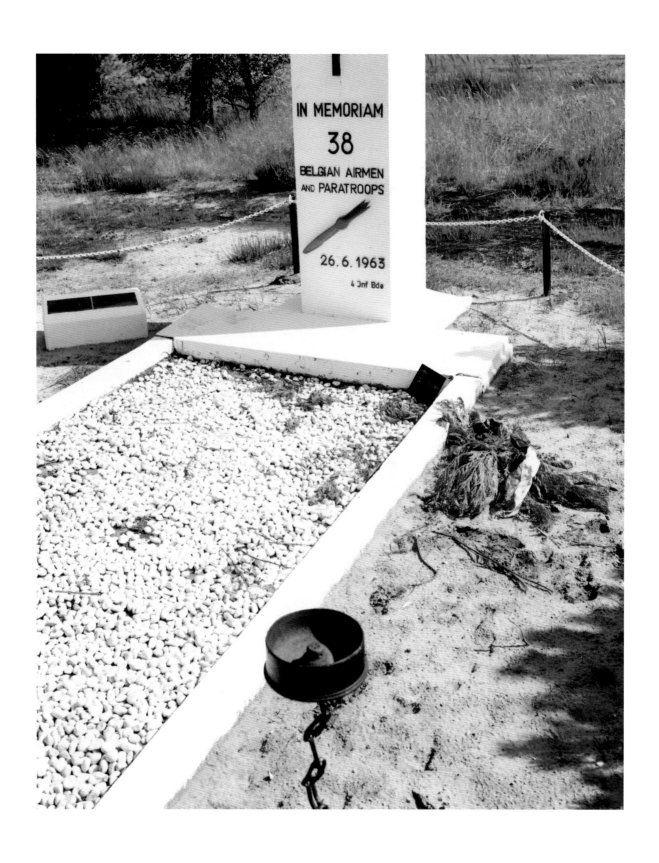

IN MEMORIAM
38
BELGIAN AIRMEN
AND PARATROOPS

26.6.1963

4 Jnf Bde

Gedenkstein für den versehentlichen Abschuß
einer Militärmaschine, die sich im gesperrten
Luftraum über der Senne befand

Memorial stone placed following
the accidental shooting down of
a Belgian military aircraft

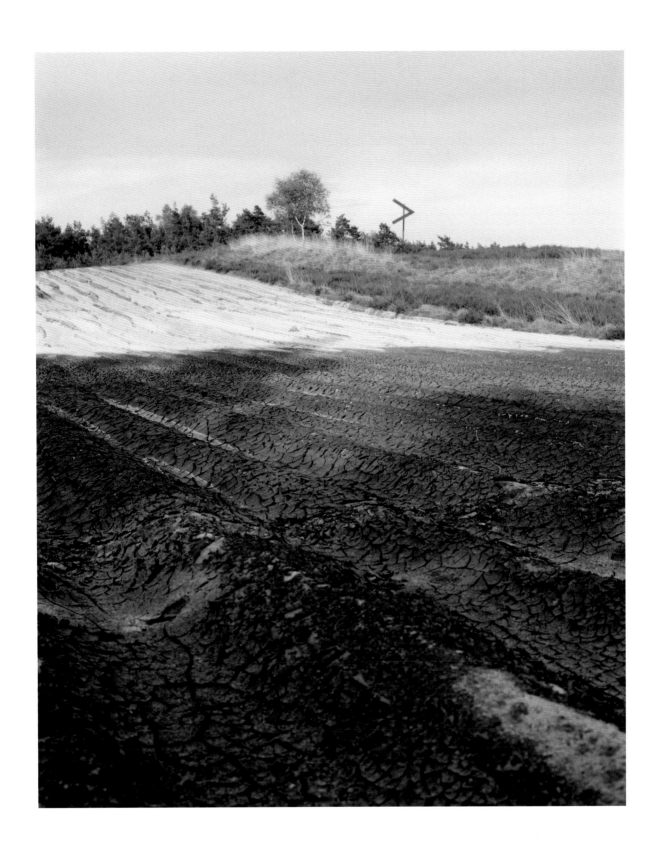

Brandschutzschneise an der Golf-Bahn | Fire break on Golf Field Firing Area

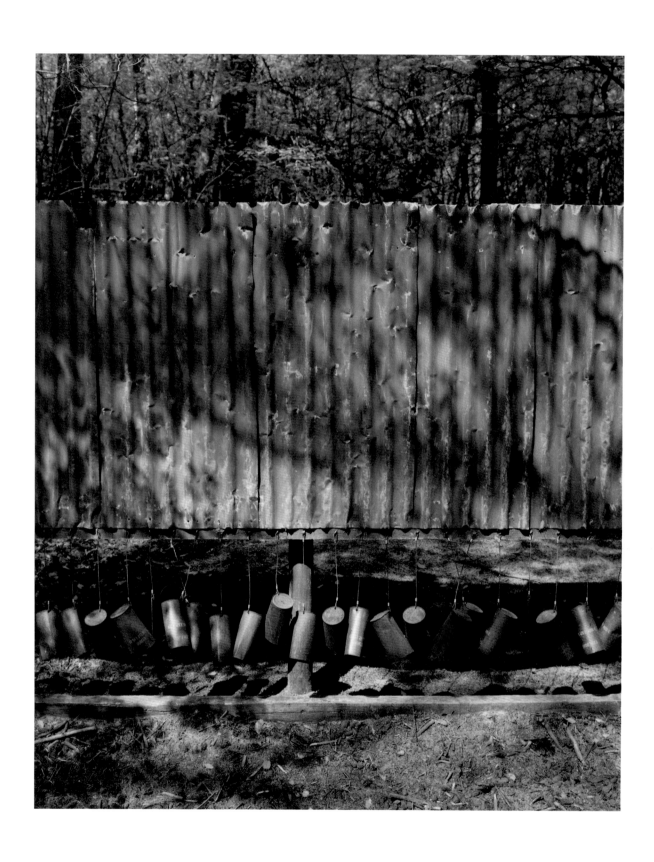

Hindernis auf der
Nachtkampfbahn Hannover

Obstacle on
Hanover Night Movement Course

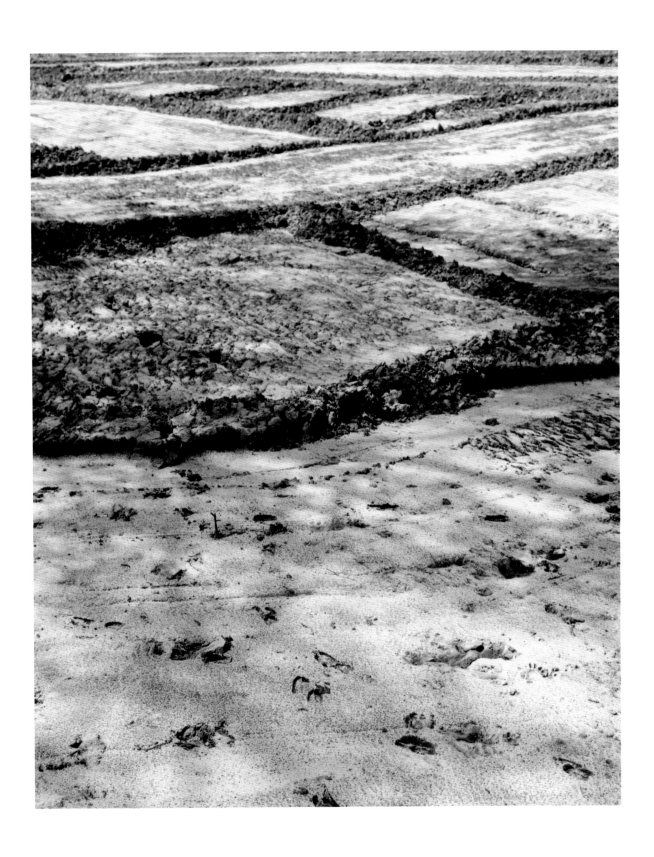

Übungsgelände zum Abschleppen von
im Kampf beschädigten Fahrzeugen

Winching Area. Exercise Area for practising
recovery of battle damaged armoured vehicles

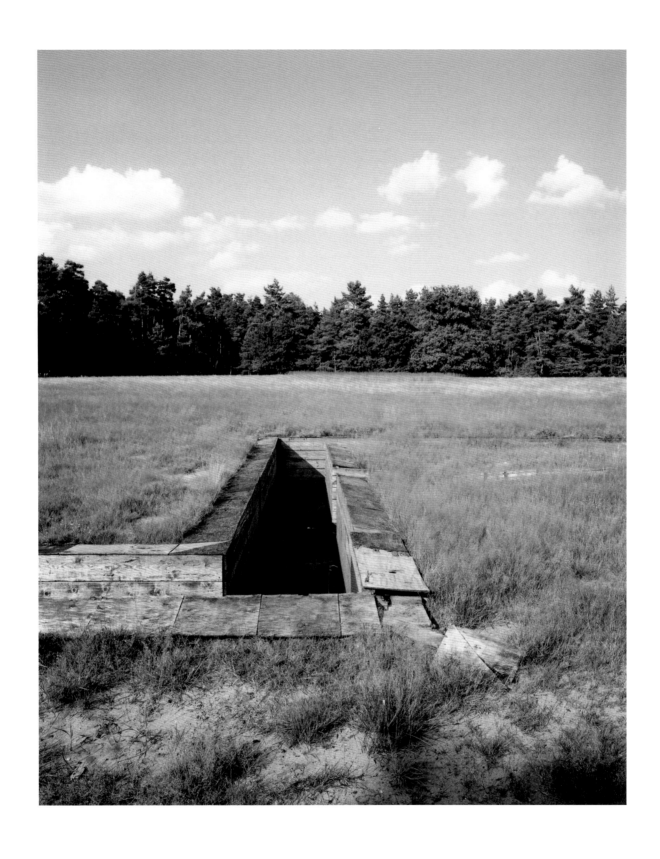

Schützengraben nach
Luftbildaufnahmen zur Vorbereitung
für den Einsatz im Golfkrieg

Iraqi Trench. Mock-up infantry trench
based on aerial photographs
used in training for the Gulf War

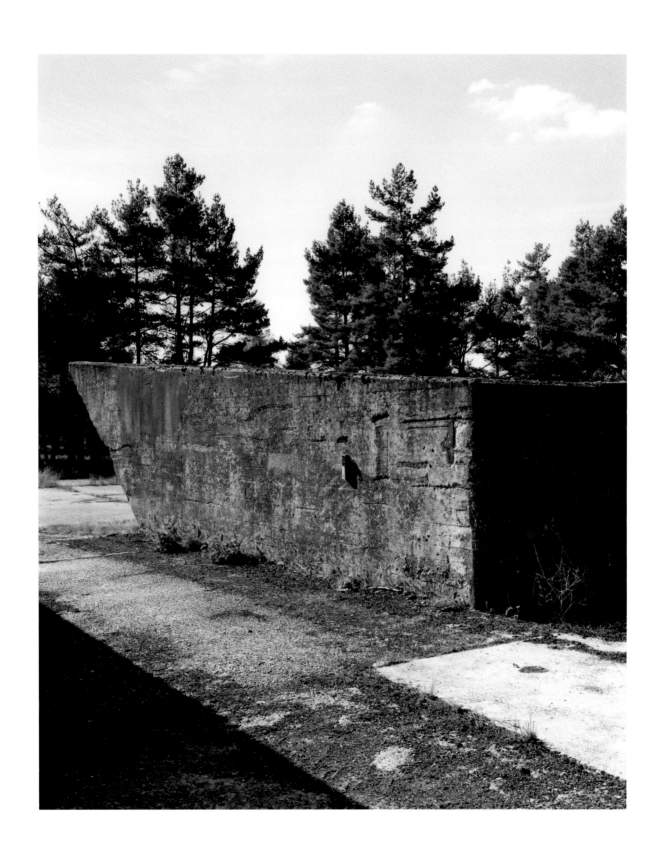

Korea-Schiff: Landungsanlage
für Panzer und Mannschaften zur
Vorbereitung für den Einsatz im Koreakrieg

Korea Ship. Concrete training mock-up
of a landing ship to train men
deploying to the Korean War

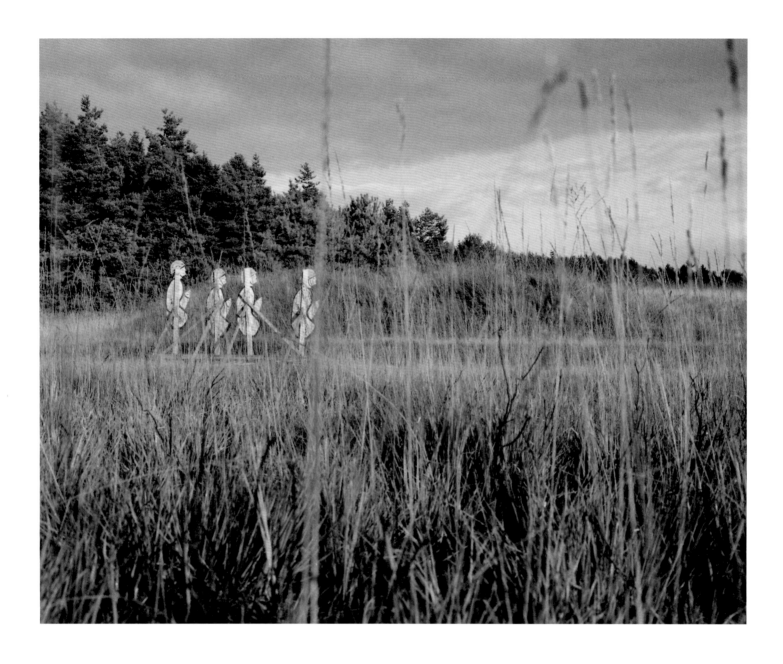

44       Spähtrupp-Attrappen auf der Oscar-Bahn | Recce troop training aid on Oscar Field Firing Area

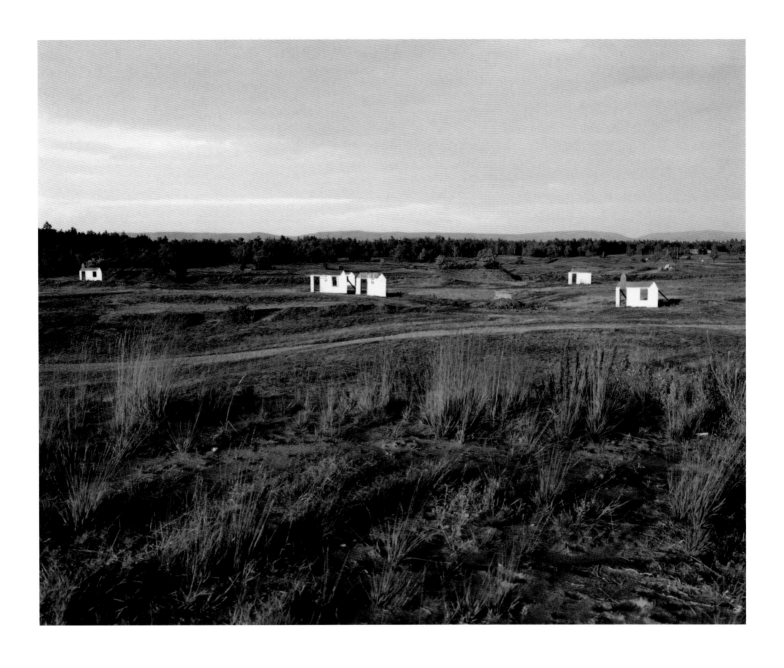

Häuserattrappen auf der Golf-Bahn | House facades on Golf Field Firing Area | 45

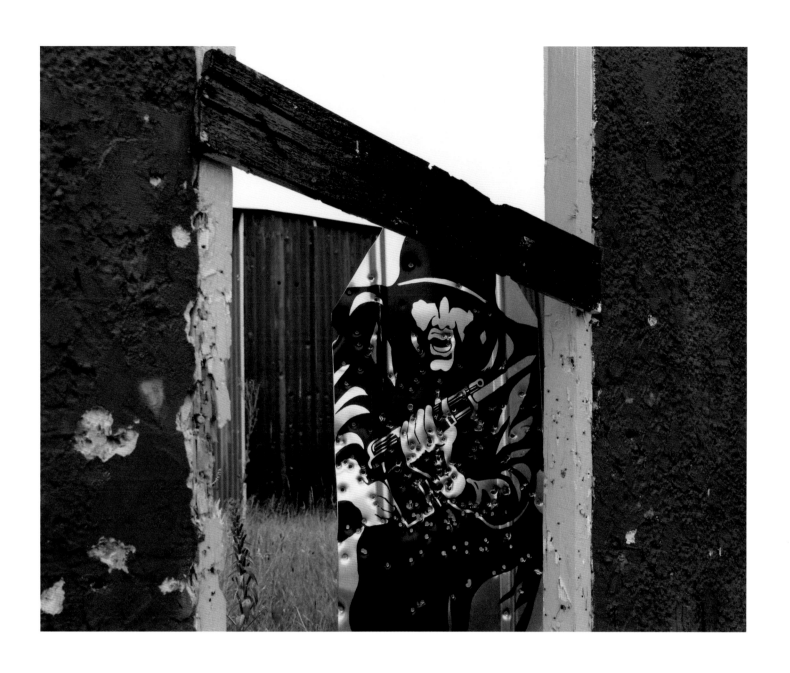

Nahkampfbahn, angreifender Soldat   |   Close Quarters Battle Range, attacking soldier      47

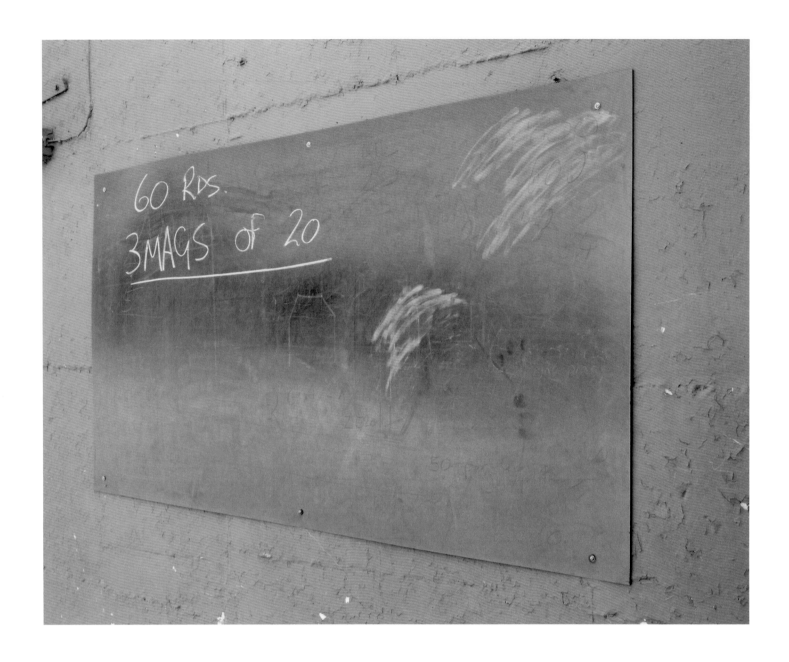

Munitionsausgabe auf Alma 2:
Schulschießbahn für Gewehr

Ammunition Issue Point on Alma 2.
Small Arms Classification Range

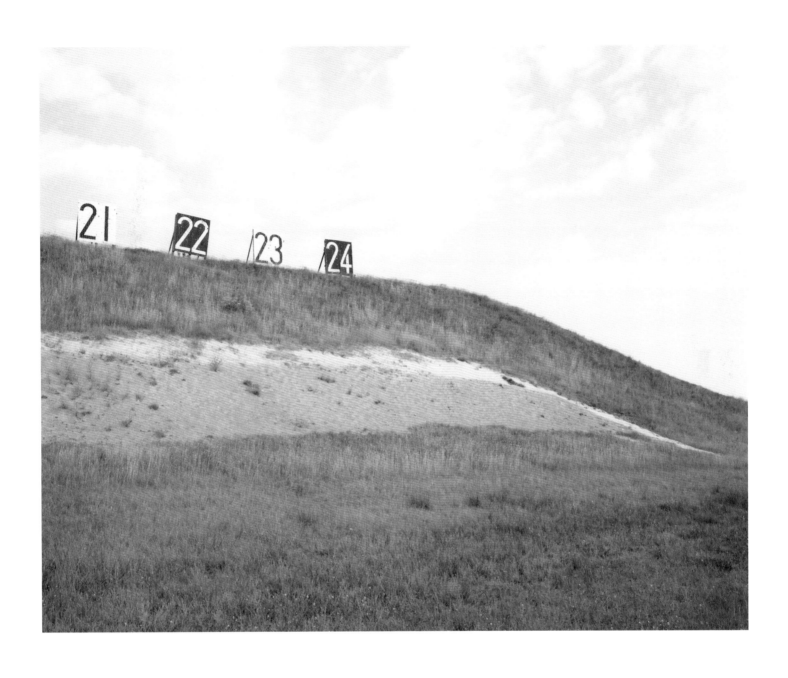

Kugelfang der Delta-Galerie,
als Sondermüll zu entsorgen

Bullet Catcher on Delta Gallery,
the content is cleared as special waste

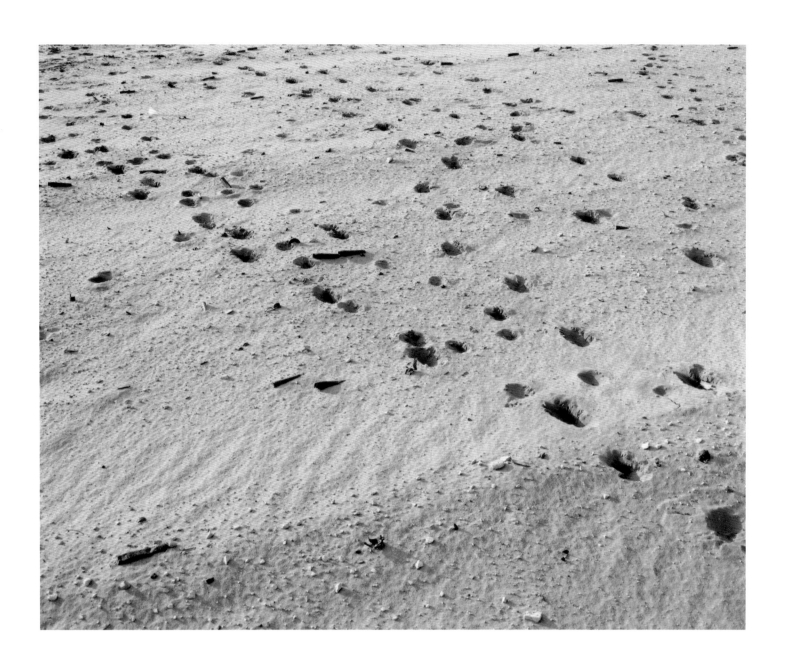

Milan-Feuerstellung auf der Lima-Bahn   |   Milan Fire Position on Lima Field Firing Area   51

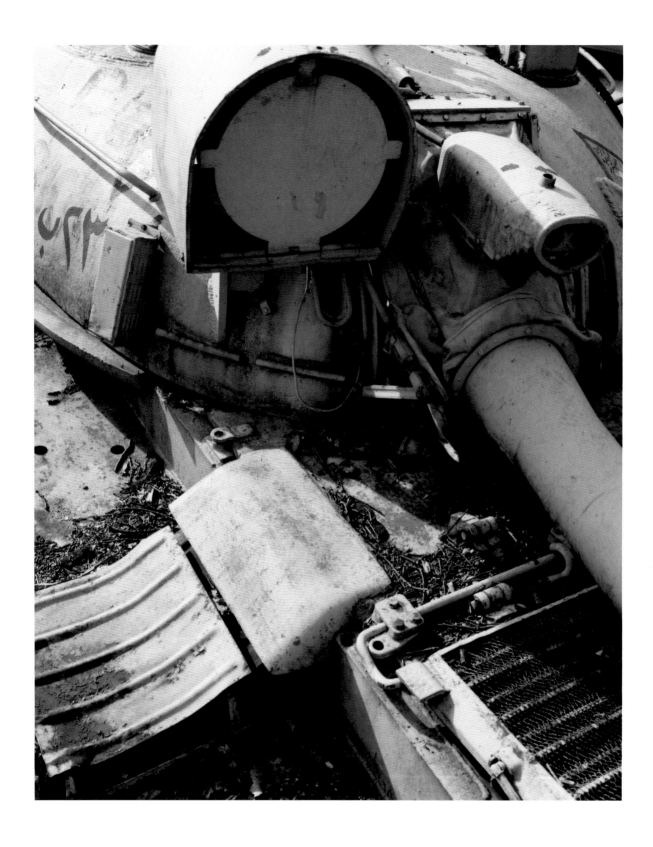

Irakischer Beutepanzer | Booty from Gulf War, Iraqi tank

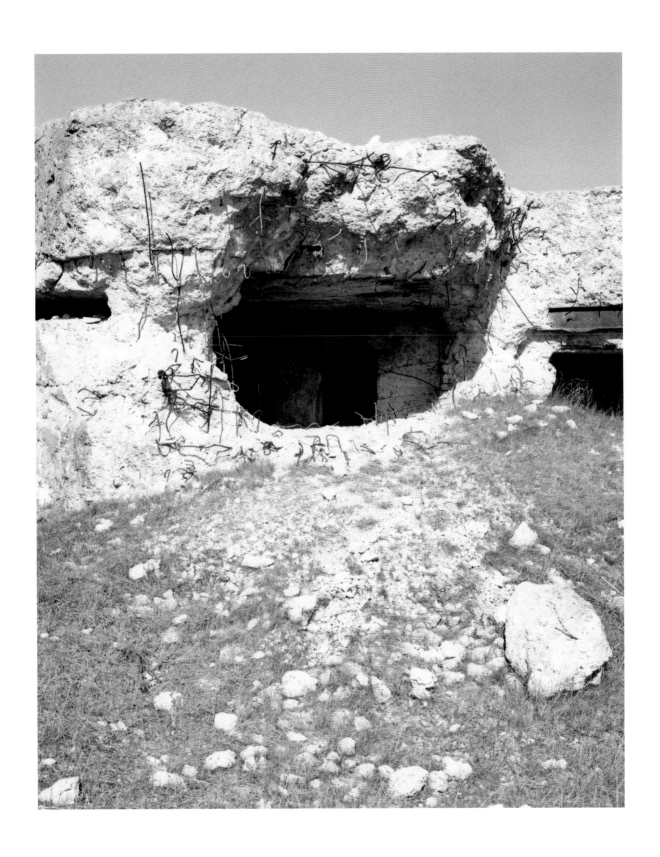

Bunker aus dem 2. Weltkrieg auf der Lima-Bahn | WW II bunker on Lima Field Firing Area

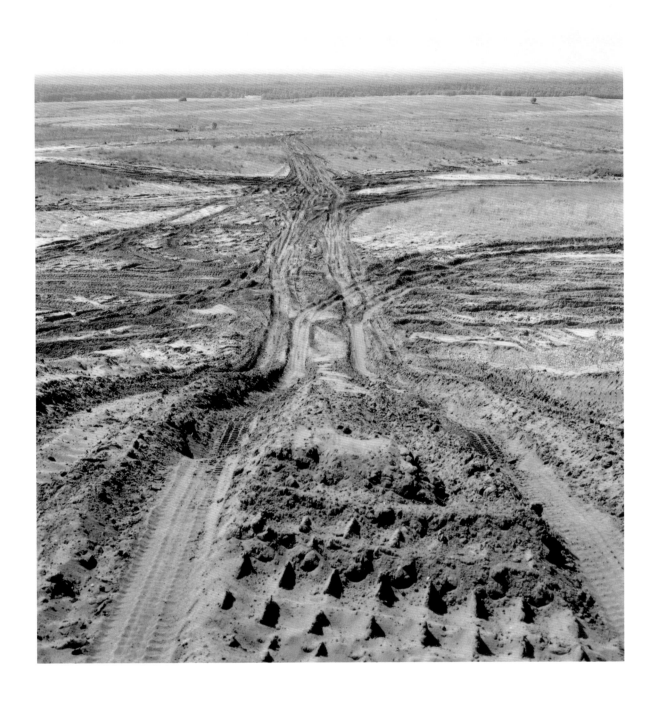

Panzerübungsgelände Stapel | Armoured Vehicle Training Area, Stapel

Green, Sennelager Golfclub | Green, Sennelager Golf Club

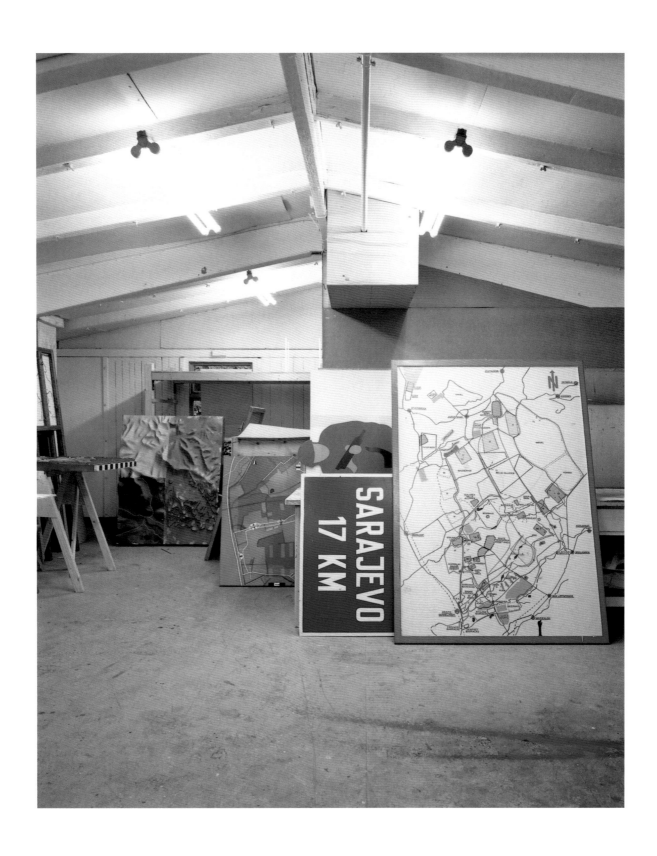

Modellabteilung der Normandy Barracks
in Sennelager

Model Maker's Department in Normandy
Barracks, Sennelager

Von Biologen mit Trassierband abgesperrte
Orchideenwiese zwischen Panzerstraße
und Zaun des Munitionsdepots 90

Orchids marked off with tape by biologists
between the military ring road and
the fence of ammunition storage area 90

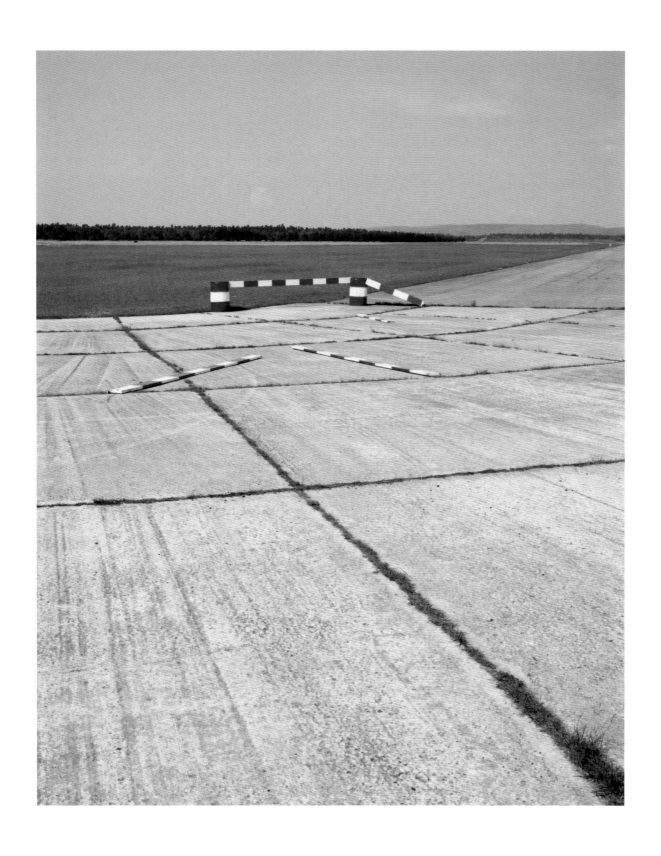

Paradeplatz an der Winning-Mühle:
Königin Elisabeth II. inspizierte dort 1965 und
1977 die Truppen der Britischen Rheinarmee

Parade ground at the Winning Mill where
HM Queen Elizabeth II. inspected BAOR troops
in 1965 and 1977

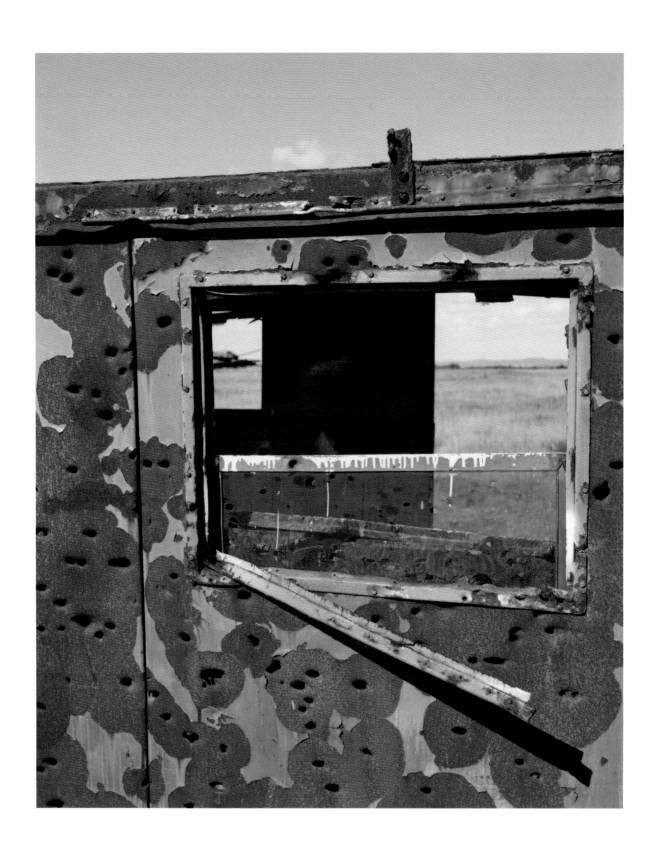

Zielpunkt auf der Bravo-Bahn:
LKW-Aufbau, außen

Target on Bravo Field Firing Area,
box body from outside

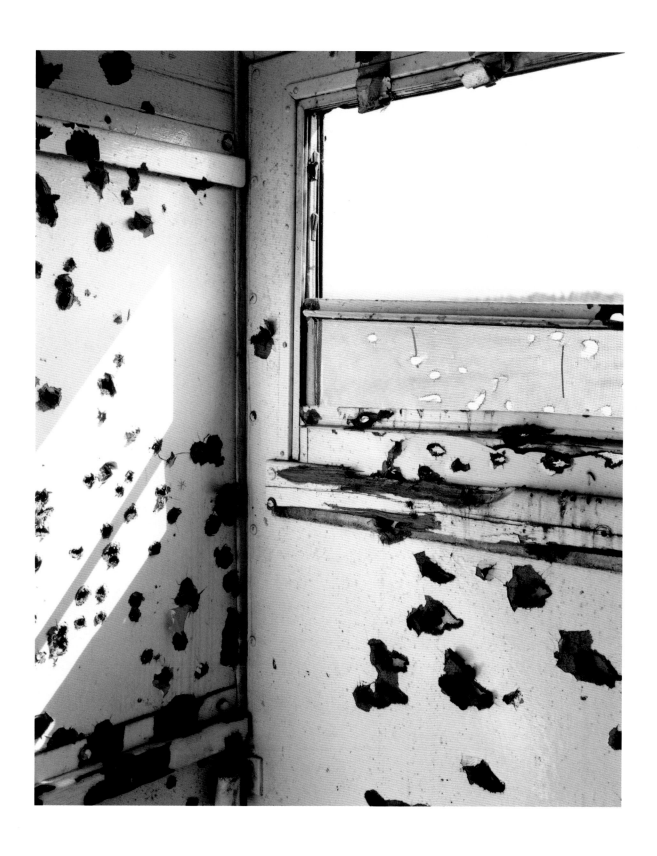

Zielpunkt auf der Bravo-Bahn: | Target on Bravo Field Firing Area,
LKW-Aufbau, innen | box body from inside

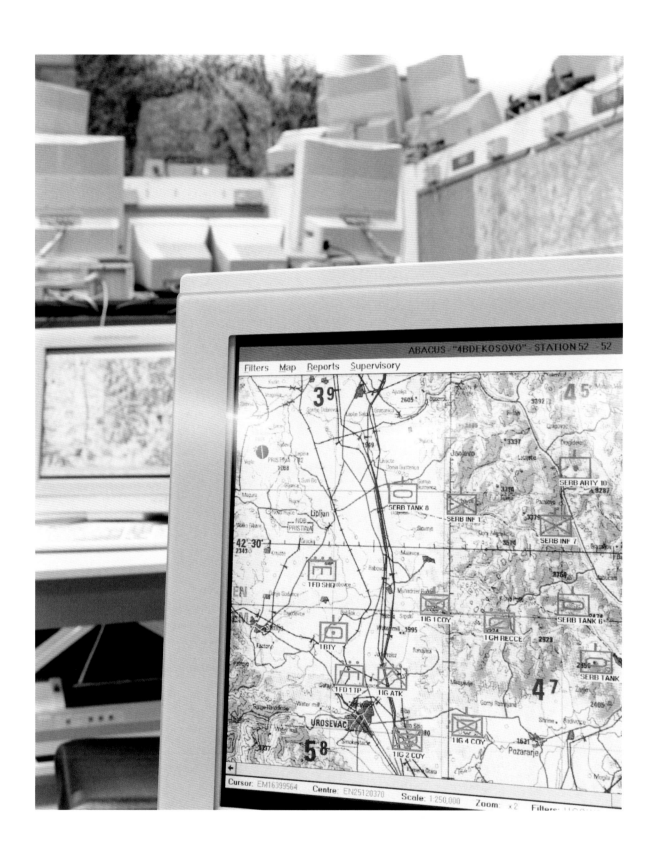

Computerzentrum zur Simulation
von Kriegshandlungen als
Vorbereitung für den Einsatz im Kosovo

Combat Manoeuvre Simulation Centre,
simulation of battle field tactics
as a scenario for action in Kosovo

## Dorf

Village

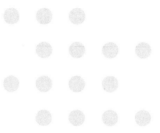

Tafel für Planspiele zum Orts- und Häuserkampf
im Übungsdorf Tin-City

Layout for operations
in the training village, Tin-City

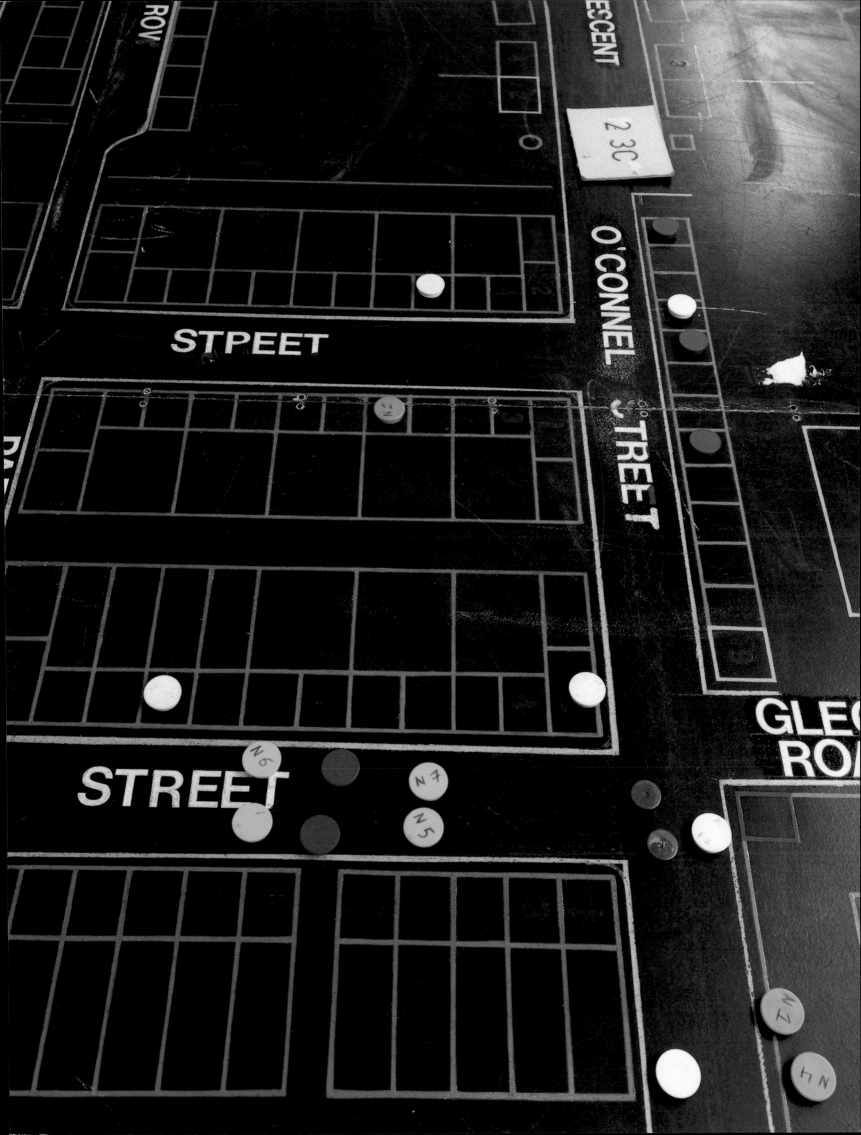

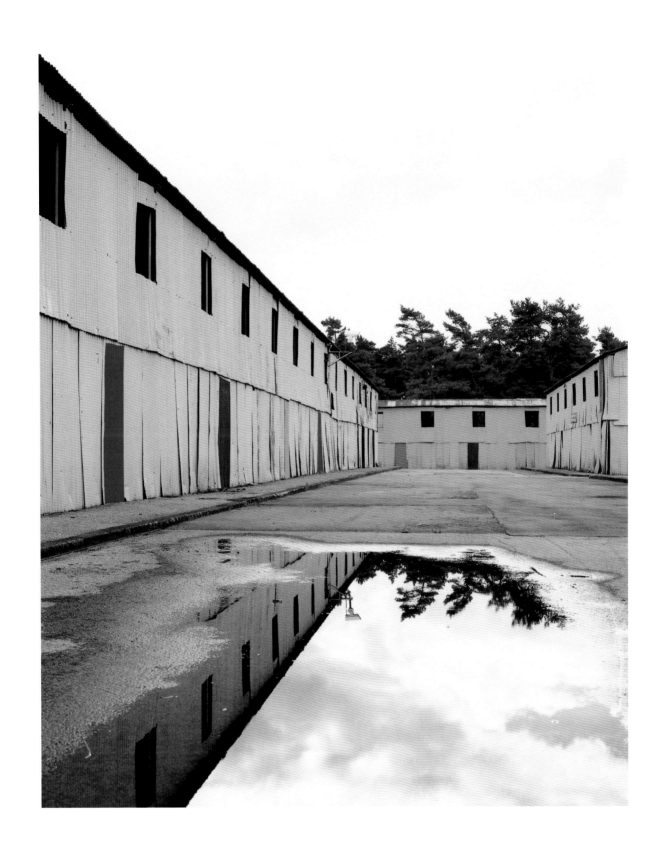

Tin-City, Wellblech-Häuserfronten
aus den 70er Jahren

Tin-City, corrugated tin
house fronts from the 1970's

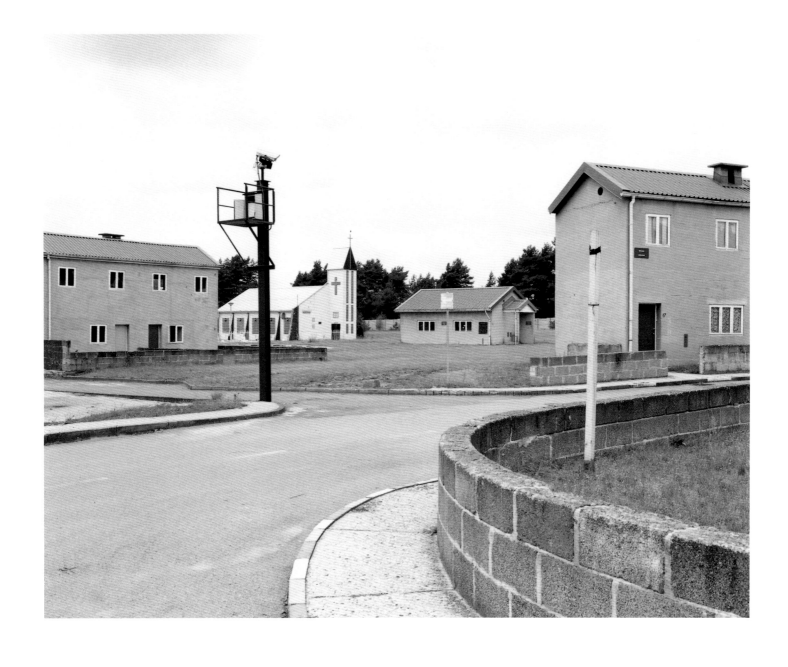

Tin-City, Steinhäuser aus den 80er Jahren | Tin-City, breeze-block houses from the 1980's

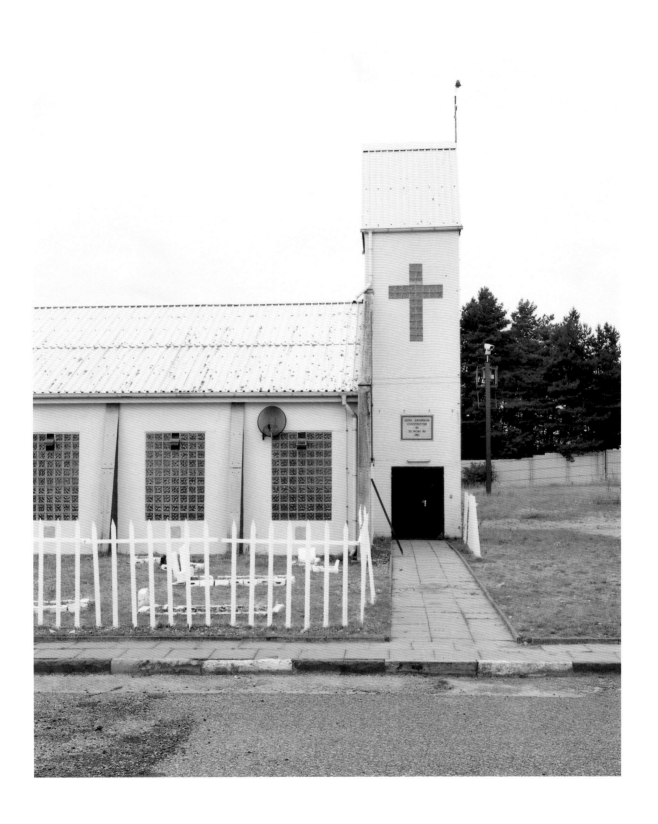

Tin-City, Soldatenkantine | Tin-City, soldiers' canteen

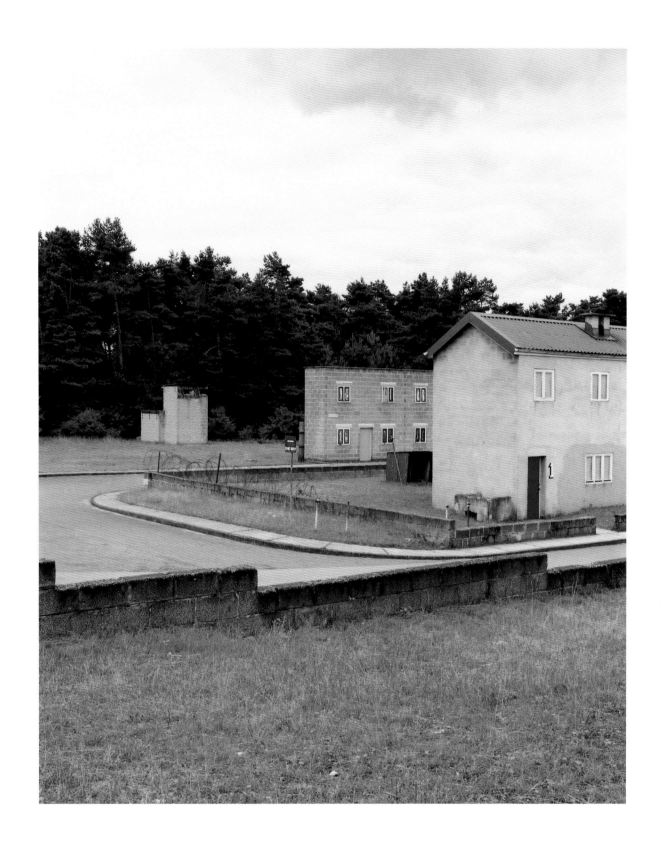

Tin-City, am Dorfrand | Tin-City, outside the village

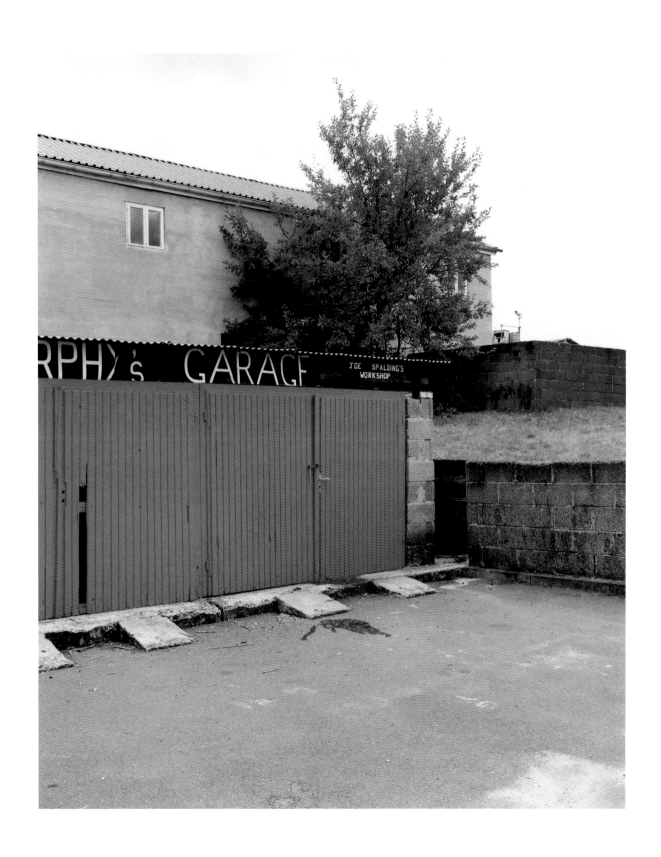

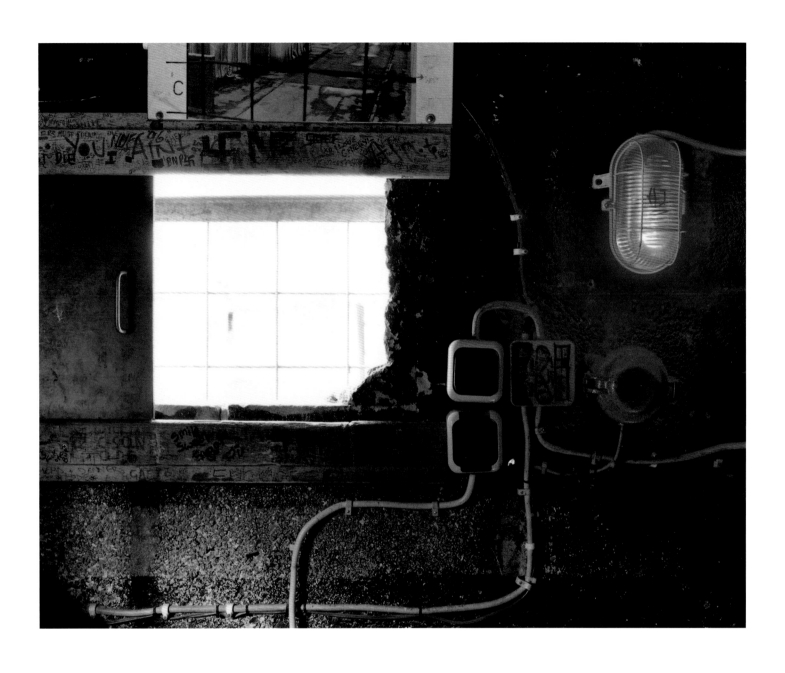

Tin-City, Wach- und Kontrollposten | Tin-City, guard post

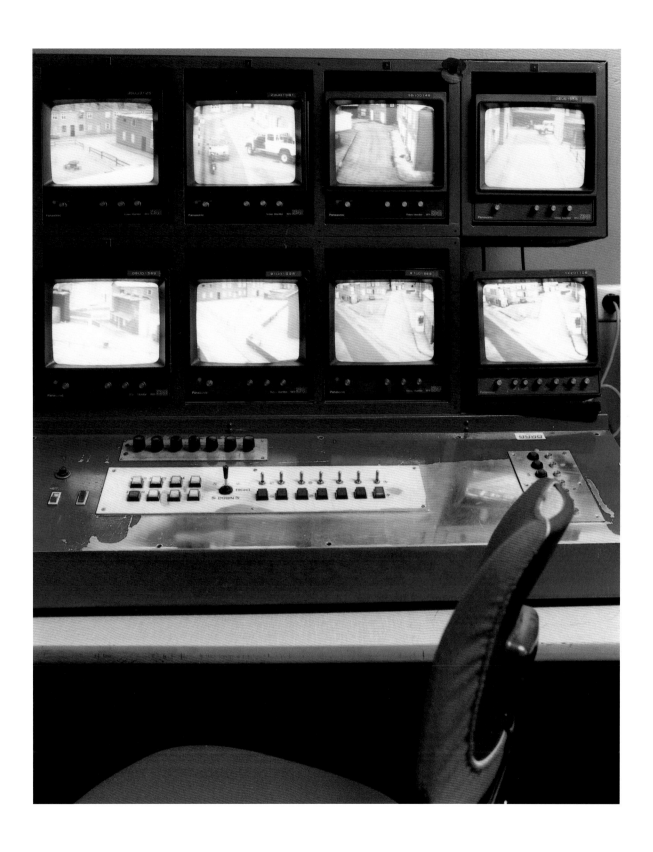

Videowand im Beobachtungsturm der
Nahkampfbahn für scharfe Munition

Closed circuit TV display overseeing
Close Quarters Battle Range

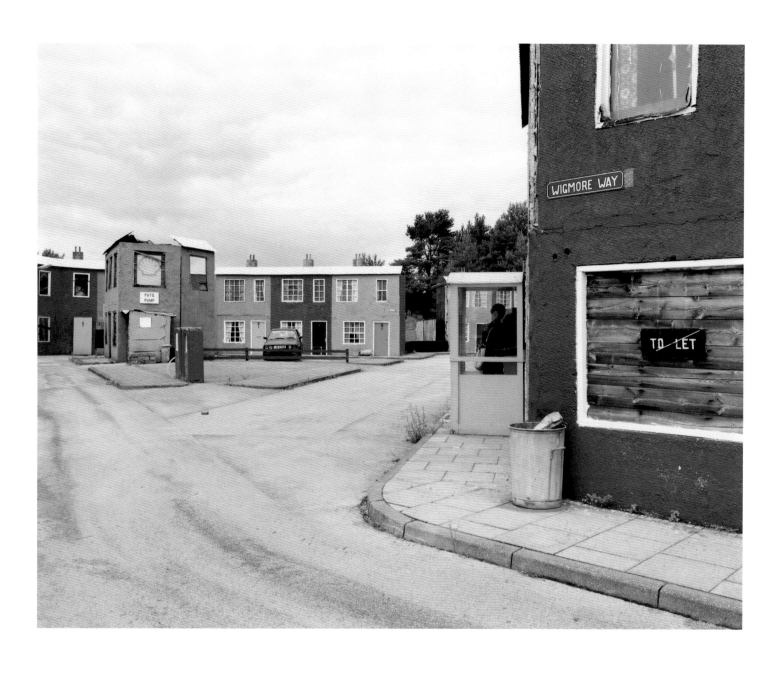

Nahkampfbahn, Dorfplatz | Close Quarters Battle Range, village centre

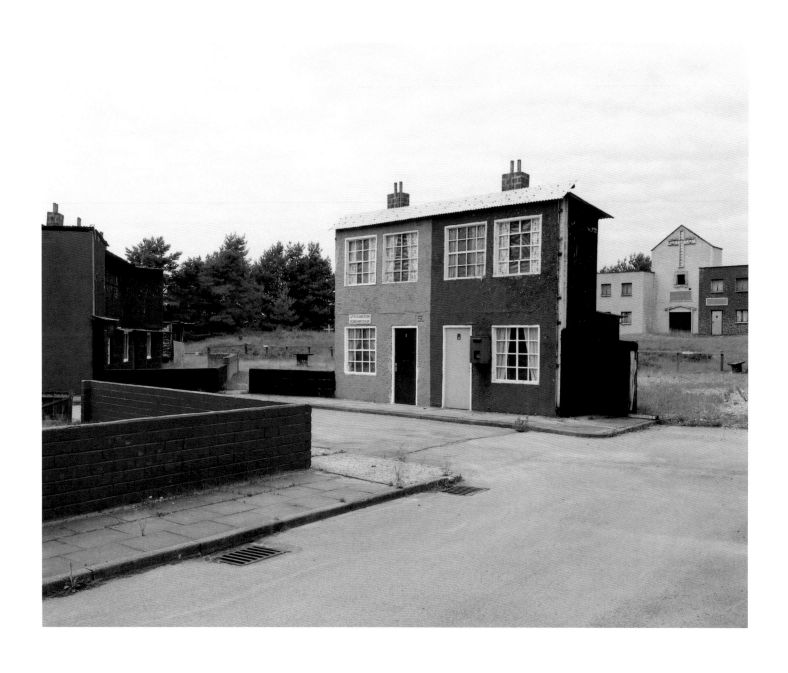

Nahkampfbahn,
Dorfstraße mit Kirche

Close Quarters Battle Range,
village centre with church

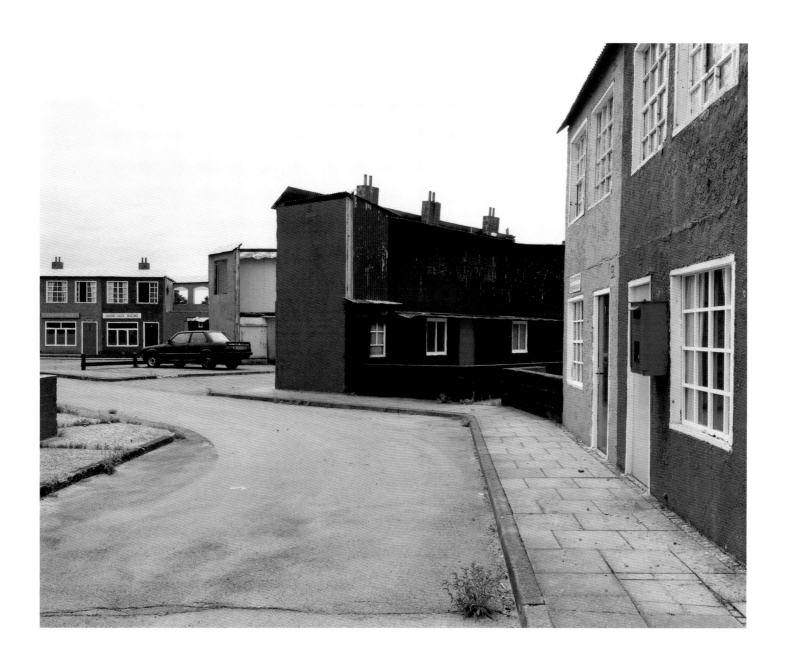

Nahkampfbahn,　　　Close Quarters Battle Range,　　　85
Dorfstraße mit PKW　　village centre with car

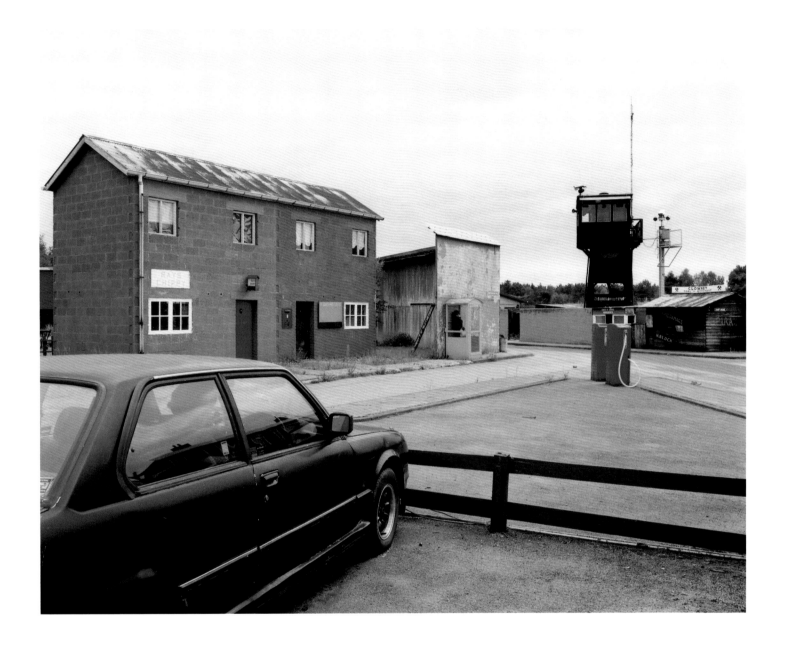

Nahkampfbahn,
Dorfplatz mit Beobachtungsturm

Close Quarters Battle Range,
village centre with observation tower

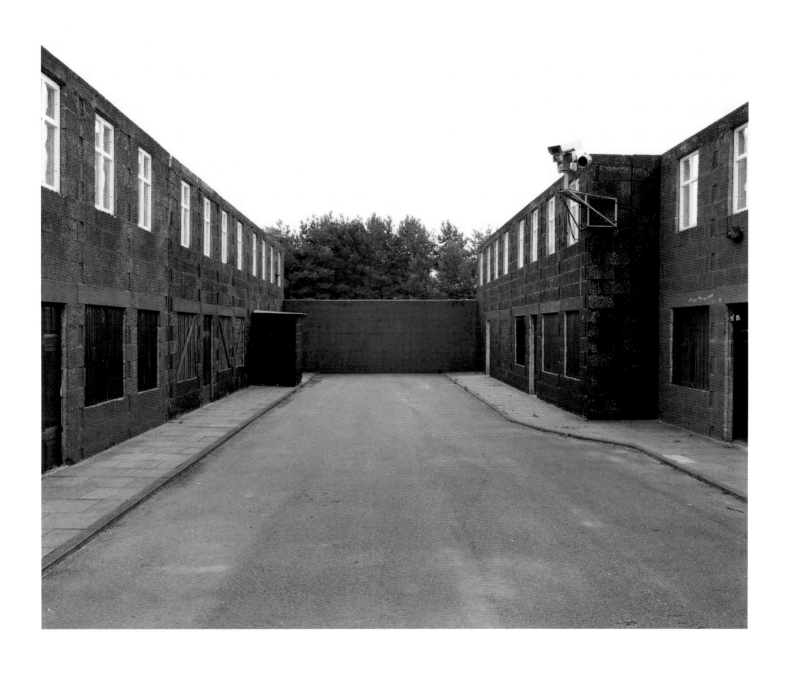

Nahkampfbahn, Sackgasse | Close Quarters Battle Range, dead end street

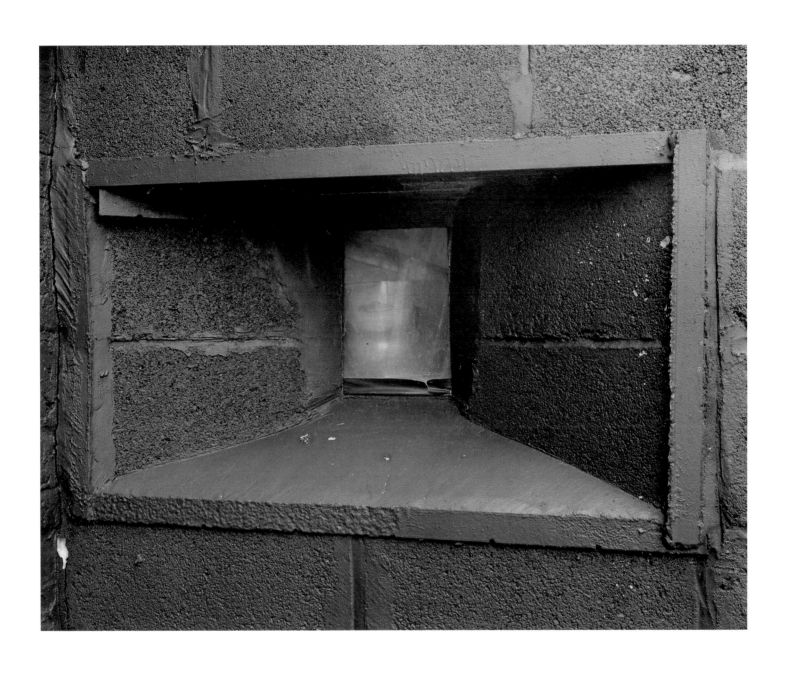

Nahkampfbahn, Bunker | Close Quarters Battle Range, bunker

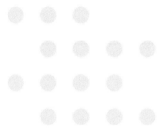

Nahkampfbahn, junge Frau
mit Kinderwagen auf Laufschienen

Close Quarters Battle Range,
young woman with pram on rails

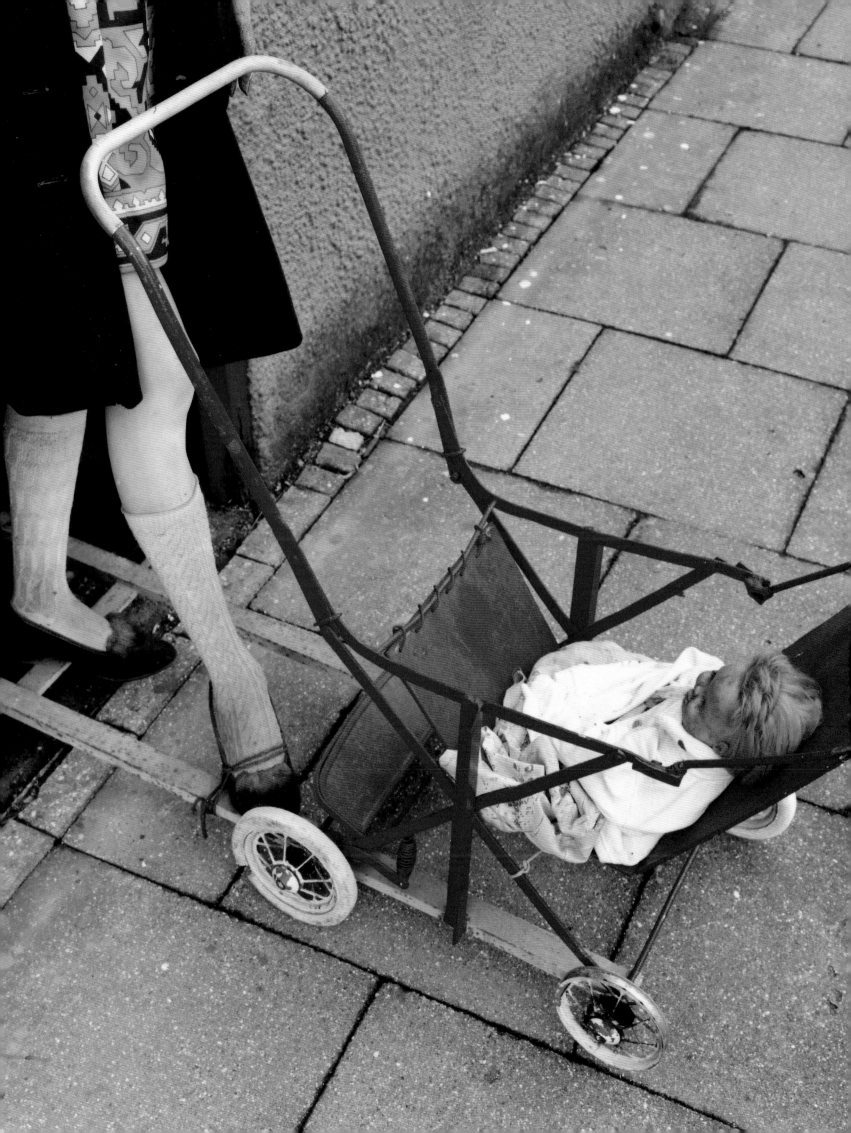

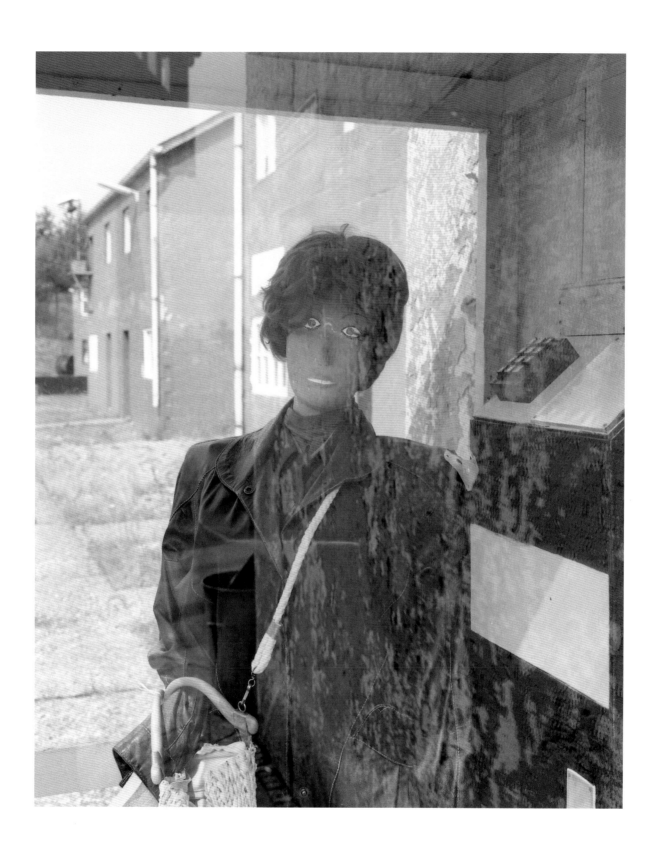

Nahkampfbahn,   |   Close Quarters Battle Range,      95

Frau in Telefonzelle       woman in telephone box

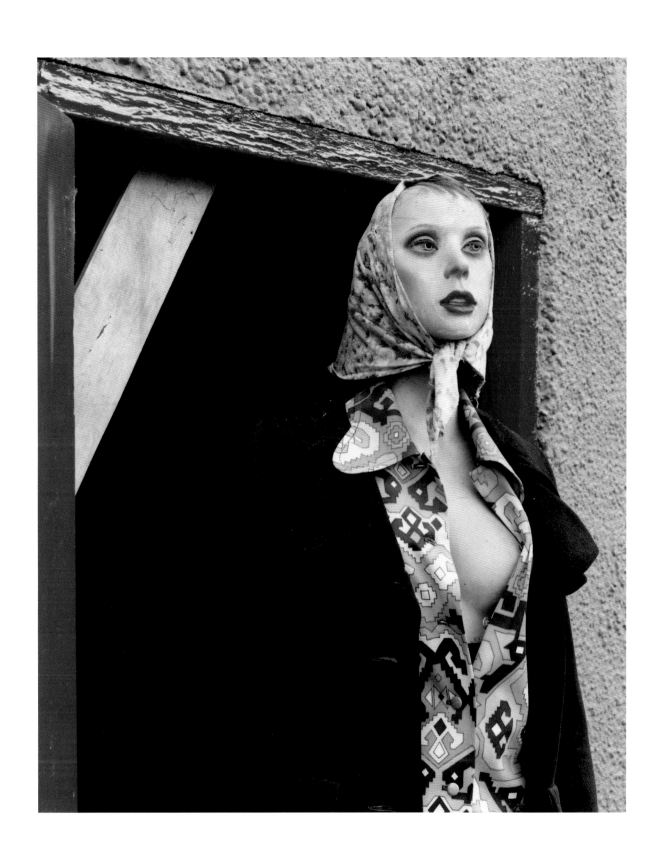

Nahkampfbahn, | Close Quarters Battle Range,     97
junge Frau in Haustür | young woman in a doorway

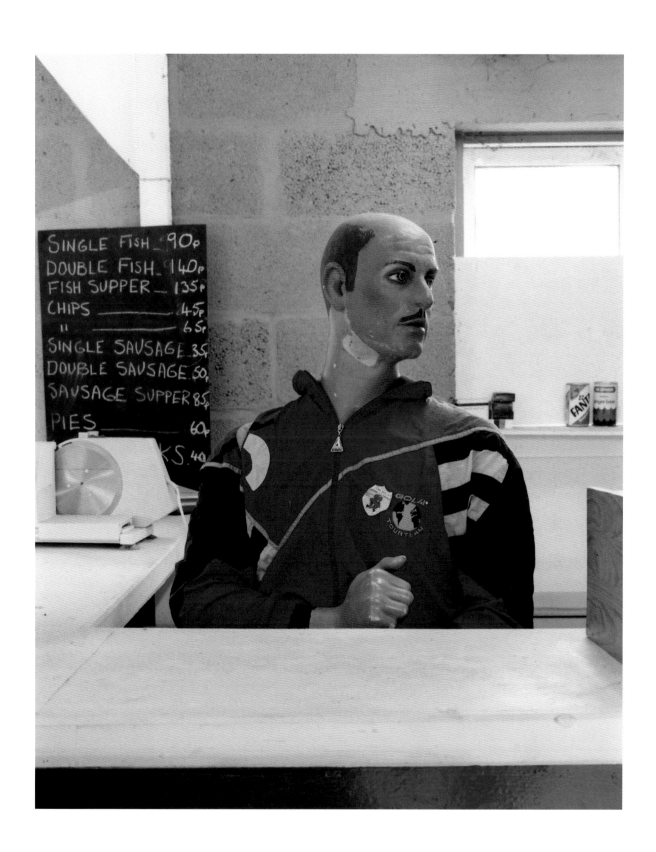

SINGLE FISH — 90ₚ
DOUBLE FISH — 140ₚ
FISH SUPPER — 135ₚ
CHIPS ———— 45ₚ
" ———— 65ₚ
SINGLE SAUSAGE 35ₚ
DOUBLE SAUSAGE 50ₚ
SAUSAGE SUPPER 85ₚ
PIES ———— 60ₚ
KS. 40

Nahkampfbahn, | Close Quarters Battle Range,
Imbißbude | fish and chip shop

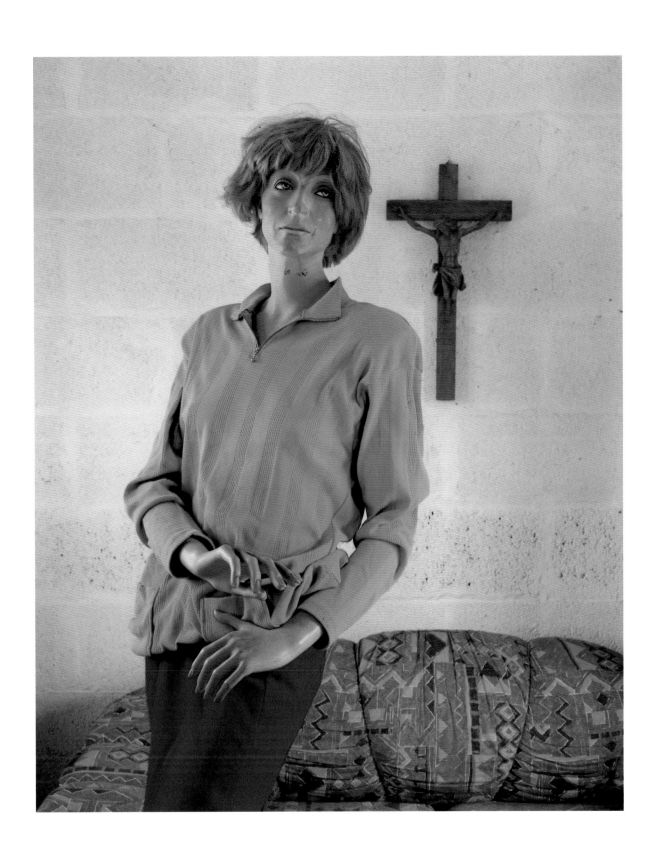

Nahkampfbahn,   |   Close Quarters Battle Range,       101

Frau mit Kreuz   |   woman with crucifix

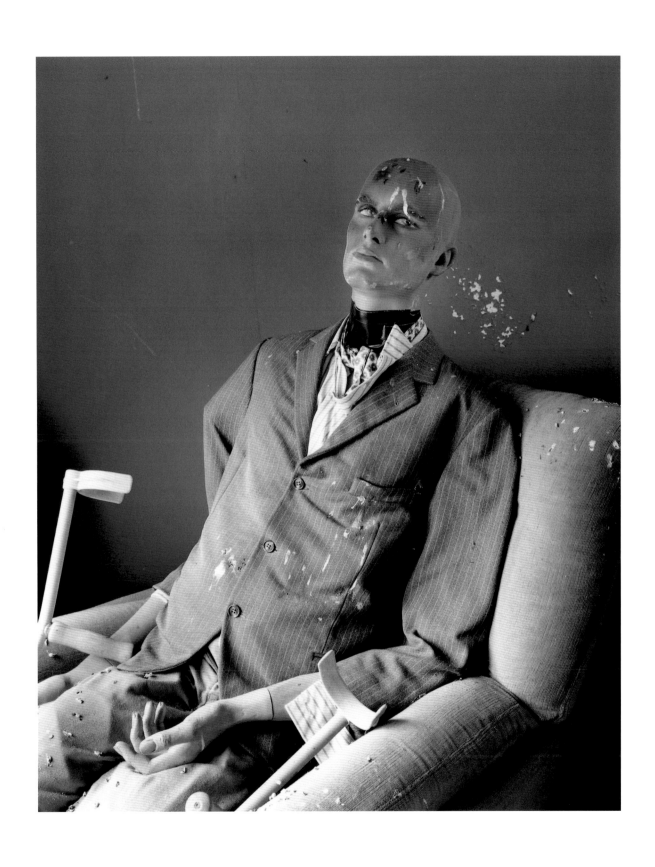

Nahkampfbahn,          Close Quarters Battle Range,
Mann mit Krücken       man on crutches

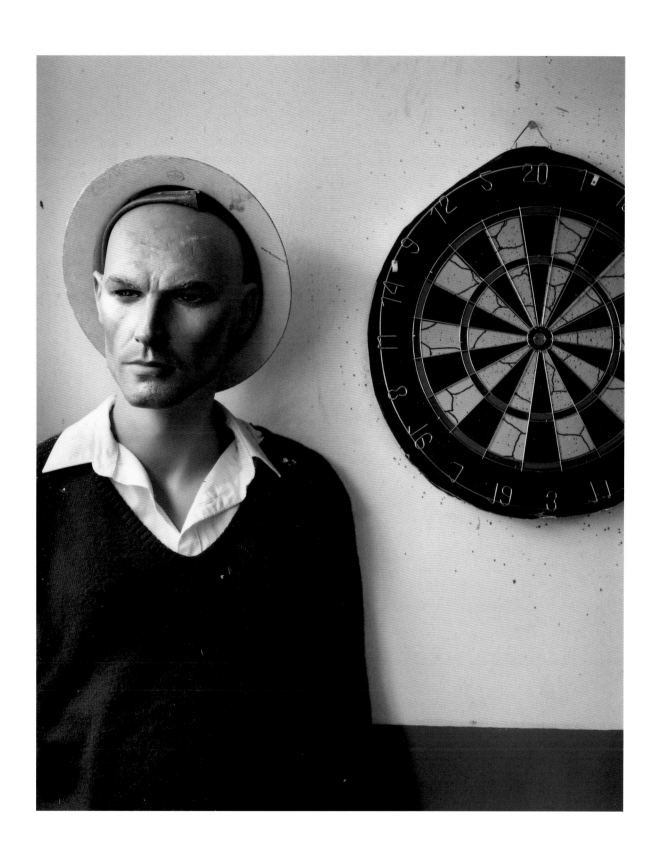

Nahkampfbahn, | Close Quarters Battle Range, |
Mann neben Dartscheibe | man beside dart board

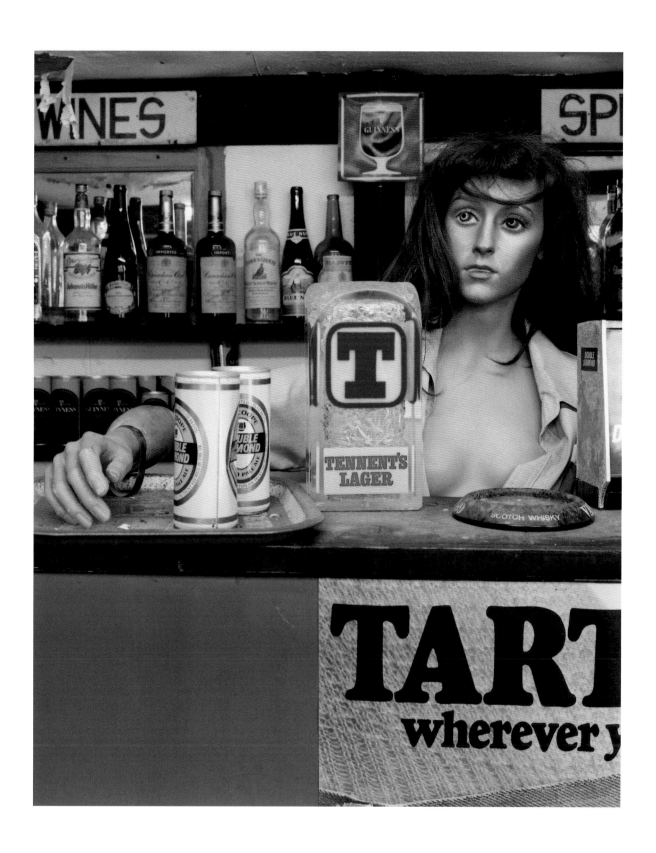

Nahkampfbahn, Bardame | Close Quarters Battle Range, barmaid | 107

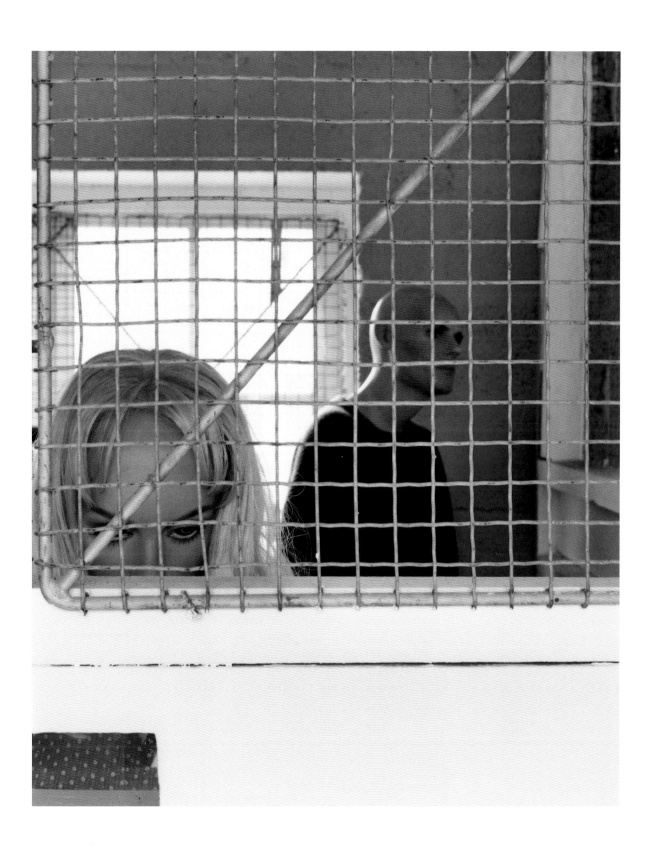

Nahkampfbahn, | Close Quarters Battle Range, 109
Postschalter | post office counter

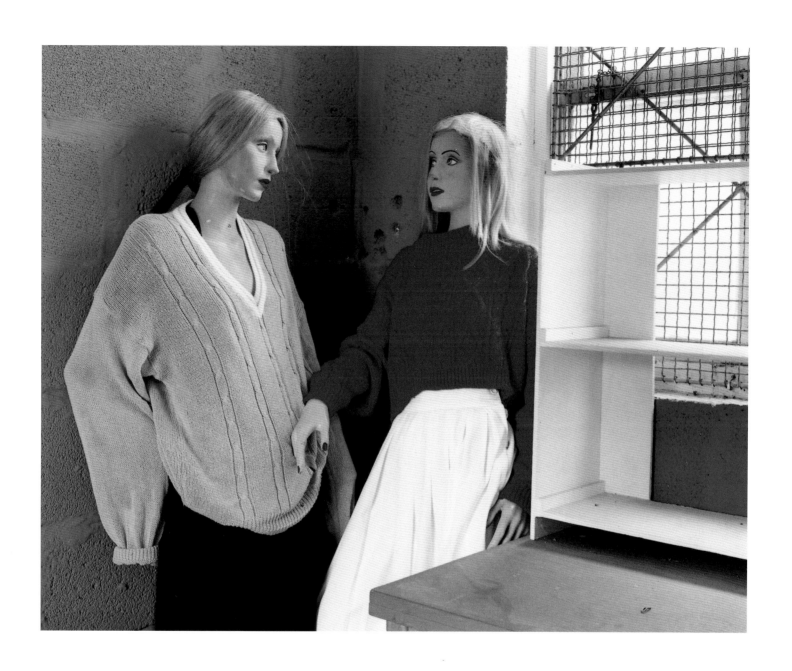

Nahkampfbahn,   |   Close Quarters Battle Range,

Jugendliche   |   Teenagers

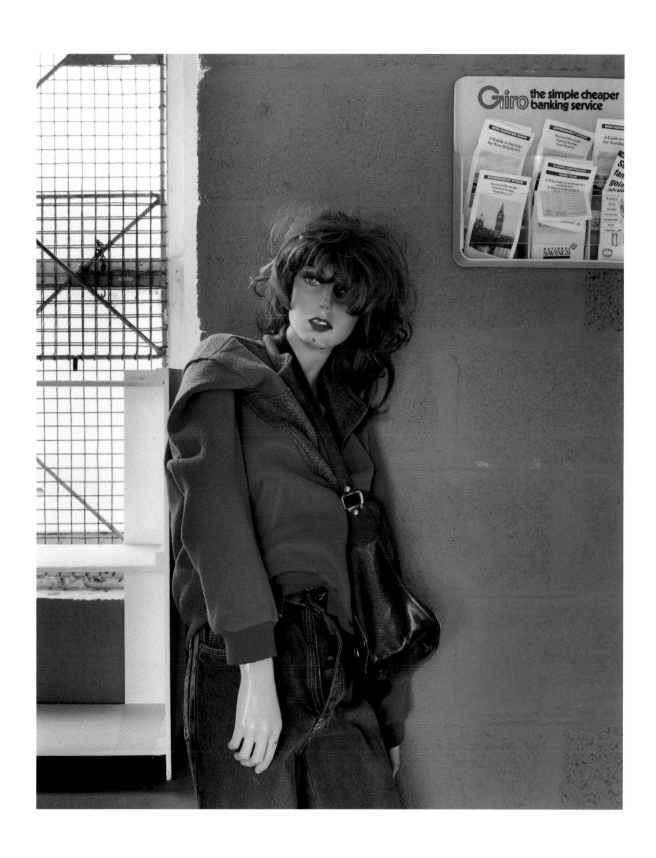

Nahkampfbahn,
Bankkundin

Close Quarters Battle Range,
bank customer

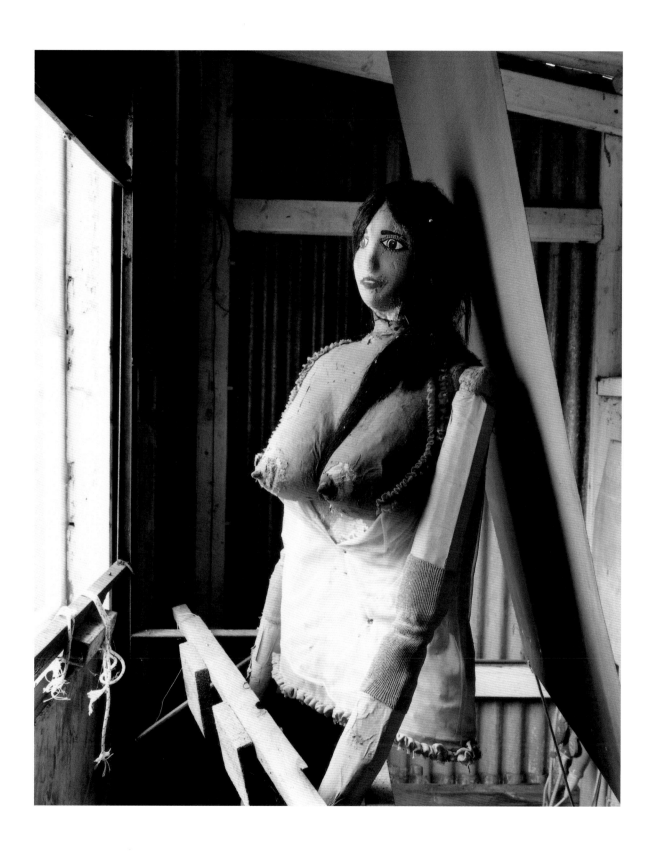

Nahkampfbahn, Prostituierte | Close Quarters Battle Range, prostitute 115

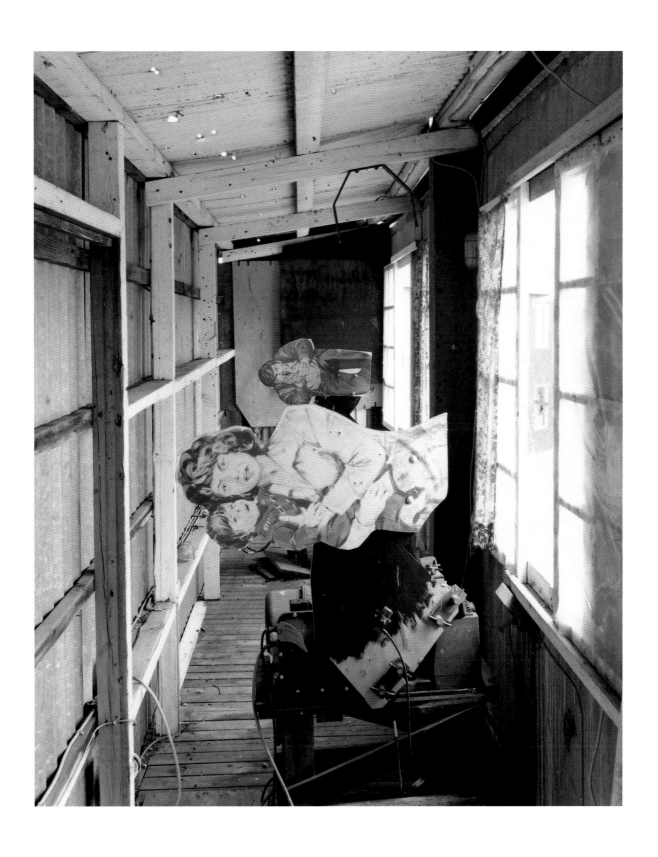

Nahkampfbahn, Mutter mit Kind
und Angreifer auf Klappscheiben

Close Quarters Battle Range, mother with child
and gunman on fall-when-hit-targets

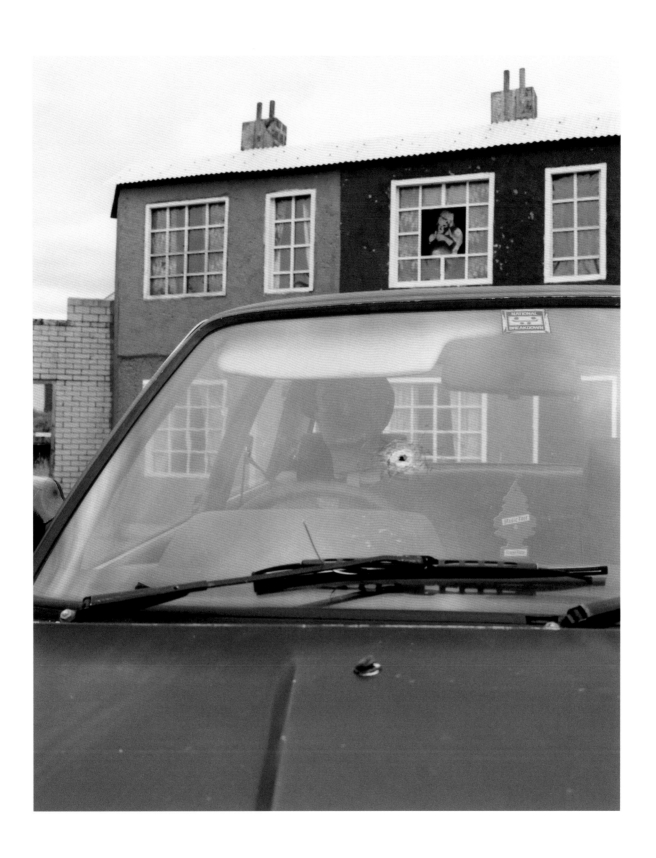

Nahkampfbahn, PKW-Fahrer | Close Quarters Battle Range, car driver

119

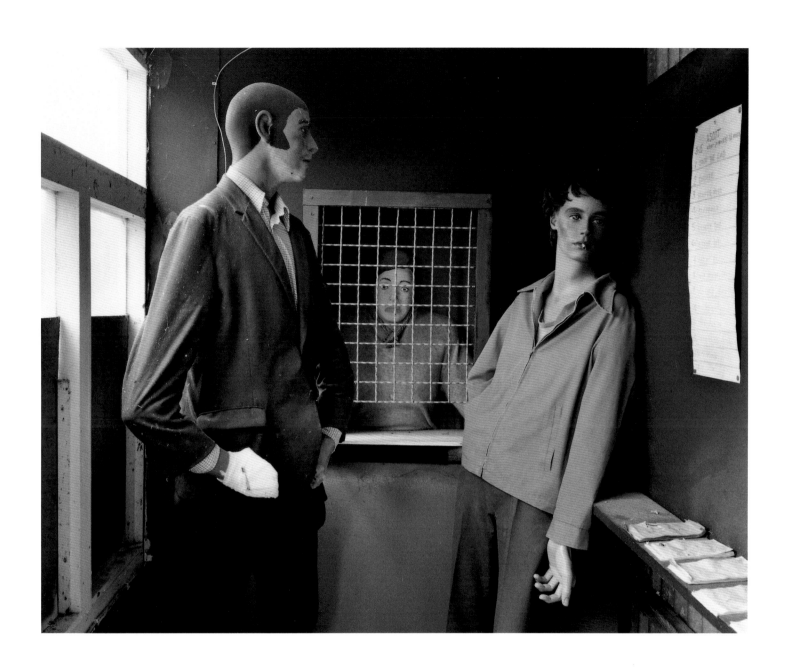

Nahkampfbahn, | Close Quarters Battle Range,
Wettbüro | betting shop

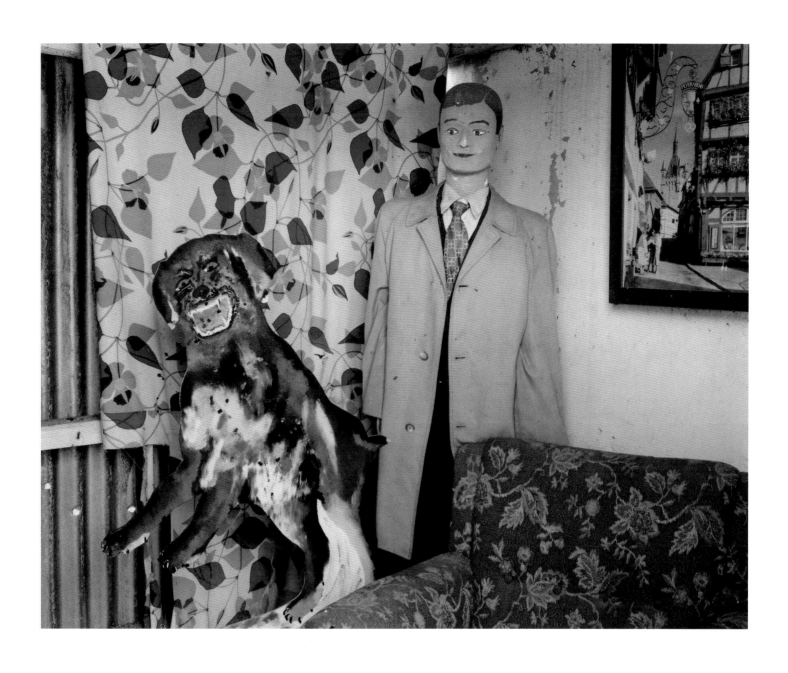

Nahkampfbahn,
Mann mit angreifendem Hund

Close Quarters Battle Range,
man with attacking dog

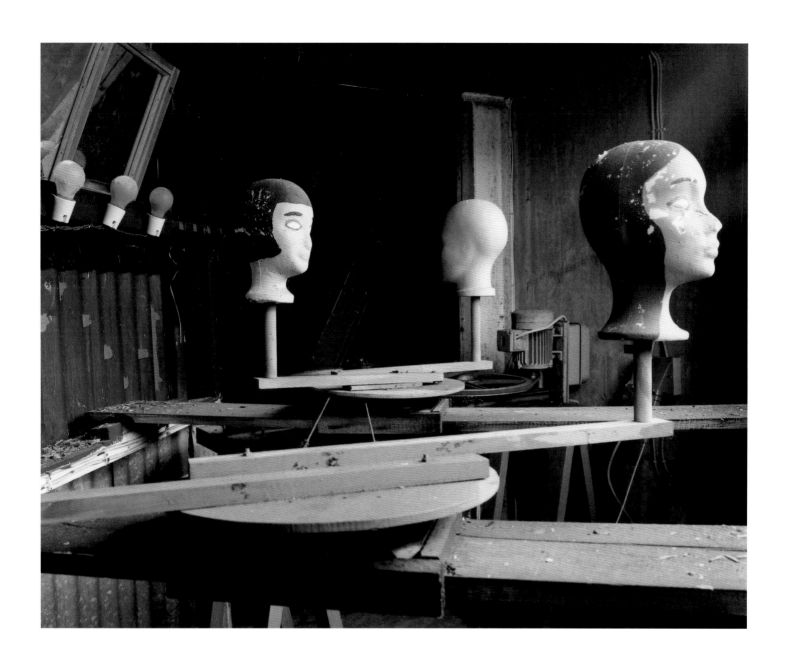

Nahkampfbahn, Disko | Close Quarters Battle Range, disco

Anna M. Eifert-Körnig

## Landschaft im Visier

## Landscape in Sights

Fotografische Erkundungen

Ein weiter Blick von oben auf eine locker bewaldete Landschaft, so weit das Auge reicht. Vom Hügel herabsteigend ist man umgeben von dem frühlingshaft satten Grün der Wiese mit kleinem Wäldchen unter blauem Himmel. Weiter voranschreitend öffnet sich dem Auge der breite Horizont der von Erika geschmückten Heidelandschaft. – Bilder unverfälschter Natur, wie wir sie durch die Hochglanzprospekte der Reiseveranstalter oder der Werbung transportiert bekommen.

Erst nach und nach entdeckt das Auge in dieser scheinbar unberührten Gegend erste Spuren von Menschen, Zeichen einer abstrakten Kartographie: rot leuchtende Schilder, Pfeiler, rätselhafte Wegweiser und Markierungen. Ein Navigationssystem, dessen verschlüsselte Symbole uns nirgendwohin führen, uns mehr verwirren als orientieren. Sie verweisen in diesem scheinbar unbevölkerten Stück Natur auf uns unbekannte Ereignisse und Vorgänge.

Unsere Sinne versetzen sich in Alarmbereitschaft. Wir hören nichts, doch der forschende Nahblick dringt immer tiefer in die Landschaft ein, und er macht, wohin wir auch vorsichtig treten, unvermutet neue Details aus. Spuren von Kettenfahrzeugen und Tieren, Patronenhülsen, zugewachsene Gräber. Silhouetten ruinenhafter Häuser, zerschossener Autos und verrosteter Panzer geben ihr Mimikrydasein nach und nach preis. Die Idylle des sonntäglichen Spazierganges ist längst dahin.

Die natürliche Landschaft verschwindet zunehmend aus dem Blickfeld. An ihre Stelle schiebt sich die von Einschüssen durchsiebte Vedute eines Schießbahnmodells. Wie durch den bemalten Vorhang eines Dorftheaters werden wir durch sie in eine verlassene Attrappenwelt geführt. Die aus Holz und Pappe provisorisch zusammengehämmerten Straßenkulissen mischen sich mit den Ruinen eines verlassenen Dorfes. Ein Feuerwehrturm ragt als Zielscheibe in die Höhe. Aus Betonplatten nachgebaute Landungsschiffe, Panzerversuchsbecken, wirklichkeitsgetreue Schützengräben und das schwarz gähnende Loch eines zerschossenen Bunkers bestätigen unser wachsendes Mißtrauen.

Plötzlich wechselt die Optik, und wir befinden uns in einem engen Innenraum; dessen durchlöcherte Mauer und der Blick auf einen fernen Panzer machen uns deutlich: Wir befinden uns inmitten eines Kriegsszenarios. Wir wissen nicht, in welchem Krieg wir sind, wer Freund und wer Feind ist. Kein Mensch ist zu sehen, wir sind allein und dennoch spüren wir die vermeintlichen Blicke in unserem Rücken: ein Zustand der Bedrohung.

Wie in der Geisterbahn lauert hier unvorhersehbare Gefahr. Die gespensterhaften Figuren, die hinter dem Fenster kampfbereit hervorblicken, auf Laufschienen plötzlich hervortreten oder auf Klappscheiben auf ihren Einsatz warten, sind letztendlich nur wie der Scheinriese in der Geschichte der Wilden 13: Aus der Ferne bedrohlich, aus der Nähe betrachtet eher bedauernswert – Täter und Opfer in einem. Man braucht allerdings zunächst Mut, sich ihnen zu nähern, um zu erkennen: Es ist doch nur ein Spiel gewesen. Ein Spiel jedoch,

## Photographic research

The view is from above down on to a lightly forested landscape as far as the eye can see: From the summit of a hill looking down and under a clear blue sky, one is surrounded by spring green meadows interspersed with small woods. Moving further, the eye is caught by the wide horizon of heathland adorned by Erika. There are images of undisturbed nature familiar to us from the glossy prospectuses of travel agents or mediated through advertising.

In this apparently undisturbed area, it is only gradually that the eye first begins to discover traces of humanity – marks of an abstract cartography; flashing red lights, arrows, mysterious signposts and marks: A navigation system, the coded symbols of which lead us nowhere, which confuse more than provide orientation. In this apparently desolate area of nature, they indicate events yet unknown to us.

Our senses are set in alarm. We hear nothing and yet, upon further penetrating exploration of the landscape, the inquiring eye inadvertently discovers new details wherever we cautiously come to step. Traces of caterpillar tracks and animals, empty bullet cartridges, overgrown graves, silhouettes of destroy-ed houses, bullet-ridden cars and rusted tanks all slowly begin betraying their imitative existence to us. The idyll of the Sunday walk has long since been abandoned.

The natural landscape increasingly disappears from sight. Gradually the vedute of a bullet-ridden shooting range inserts itself into view. Just like being led behind the painted curtain of a village theatre, we are drawn into an abandoned world of fake ob-jects. The provisional street backdrop of wood and cardboard combines with the ruins of an abandoned village. A fire watch tower looms above like a target.

A landing stage made of concrete slabs, testing pools for tanks, realistically constructed trenches and a yawning black hole of what was once a bunker all confirm our growing suspicions.

Suddenly, the view changes and we now find ourselves in a narrow interior space; its perforated wall and the sight of a tank in the distance leave us in little doubt: We are now at the centre of a war scenario. We have no idea of what war we are in and are unable to distinguish friend from foe. Nobody is in sight, we are alone and yet we sense watchful eyes at our backs: A threatening situation.

Almost as if in a ghost train, there lurks un-foreseen danger here. The ghostly figures – ready for battle and constantly on the lookout, suddenly appearing on tracks or waiting for their deployment on fold-out discs – turn out to be like the false giant in the story of "John Button and the 13 Wild Men": From a distance, they appear threatening, but from close quarters rather more pitiful – they are suspect and victim rolled into one. Initially it requires cour-age to approach them so as to confirm that it is indeed a mere game. Nevertheless, it is a game in which, as in a film, the well known opening credit appears: "The action of this story is based on events that actually occurred, the names of the protagonists have been changed by the editors".

Drawn in by the camera of Claudio Hils, the lens allows the observant eye to search the surrounding area as if through the telescopic sights of a weapon. As if on patrol, the pictures lead us through the landscape. At first, we have the distanced view from the safety of the posts, then a broader view of the unexplored area, evoking the feeling that we are at the mercy of the unknown. As our senses are already in a state of alarm, the focus now is simply on the will to survive. By lurking and

in dessen Vorspann der aus manchen Filmen wohlbekannte Hinweis gehört: „Die Handlung beruht auf wahren Gegebenheiten, die Namen der Akteure wurden von der Redaktion geändert."

In dieses Spiel werden wir durch die Kamera des Fotografen Claudio Hils verwickelt, dessen Objektiv das betrachtende Auge wie durchs Zielfernrohr eines Gewehrs die Umgebung absuchen läßt. Wir werden mit den Bildern wie auf einer Patrouille durch die Landschaft geführt. Zunächst der distanzierte Ausblick vom sicheren Posten aus, dann die weit offene Optik in einer unerkundeten Gegend, die das Gefühl des Ausgeliefertseins und der Unvorhersehbarkeit evoziert. Auf die Alarmbereitschaft der Wahrnehmung folgt die Fokussierung der Sinne um des Überlebens willen. Mit der Perspektive des Lauerns und Lauschens während des Einsatzes in den verwinkelten Straßenschluchten oder bei der Auskundschaftung des Spähtrupps im Gras befindet sich der Betrachter unmittelbar in einer Aktion zwischen Angriffslust und Bangen. Und schließlich der enge Bildraum eines rettenden Unterschlupfs, der aber das beklemmend klaustrophobische Gefühl des in die Enge Getriebenen gleichermaßen mitschwingen läßt.

Eine solch radikale Lesart der Kameraoptik der Bilder wird nicht zuletzt durch die Zweckbestimmung des Geländes ausgelöst, auf dem diese Aufnahmen entstanden sind. Das Sennelager Training Center ist seit dem letzten Jahrhundert unter verschiedensten politischen Konstellationen und Machtverhältnissen militärisches Sperrgebiet und als solches nichts anderes als Schauplatz von echten Kriegsspielen. Ein Ort der Einübung von Kampf, Gewalt und Verteidigung unter kontrollierten Bedingungen: ein Versuchsfeld des Krieges und der „Logistik der Wahrnehmung"[1].

Die hier vorgelegten Bilder sind das Ergebnis einer langjährigen „künstlerisch-fotografischen Feldforschung" von C. Hils auf diesem Gelände.

Wenn uns auch hier ein thematisch und ästhetisch homogenes Material vorliegt, so ist es nicht im Sinne einer Serie organisiert, in der die einzelnen Aufnahmen eine fest bestimmte Position in der Reihe einnehmen würden. Gewiß wird dem Betrachter durch die drei großen thematischen Blöcke – Landschaft, Dorf und Menschen – in der Ausstellung bzw. im Katalog eine bestimmte Reihenfolge nahegelegt, doch die aufgestellte Ordnung ist nicht bindend gedacht. So können wir die Freiheit genießen, nach immer neuen Zusammenhängen und Bezügen in bzw. zwischen den Aufnahmen zu suchen. Entlang einem optischen Leitfaden entfaltet sich die innere Logik der künstlerischen Dokumentation immer wieder aufs neue. Die Lesart der Geschichten entwickelt sich schließlich jeweils in der Konfrontation der gebotenen Perspektive, Optik und Raumkonstruktion der Fotos mit den Bilderfahrungen, Assoziationen und Erwartungen der Betrachter.

Bilder schießen

Die Analogie zwischen Kamera und Gewehr wurde spätestens seit den Phasenfotografien eines E. J. Mareys als solche gesehen, in visueller wie auch in technischer Hinsicht vielfach erprobt und verbal manifestiert. Die unentwirrbaren Verflechtungen des Bilderschießens wurden in jüngster Zeit nicht zuletzt durch die neuesten Medienerfahrungen vom Krieg – etwa im Irak – in den Theorien von P. Virilio und J. Baudrillard hinlänglich (und medienwirksam) analysiert. Es ist nun allzu verständlich, wenn sich auch dem Betrachter der Bilder von der Senne diese Konnotation als erstes anbietet. So legitim und offenkundig allerdings eine derartige Lesart erscheinen mag, der Betrachter sollte dennoch für weitere Erkundungen der Bilder offen sein.

Die zuvor in der Kriegsspielmetaphorik ausgelegte Kameraoptik widerspiegelt zunächst auch die im Stile des Fotojournalismus durchgeführte künstlerische

listening during operations in the narrow streets or during the reconnaissance patrol through grassland, the observer finds himself torn between the desire to attack and anxiety. Finally, we enter the photographic space of a safe shelter, which more or less perpetuates the oppressive and claustrophobic feeling of being driven into a corner.

Such a radical way of reading the images through the perspective of the camera is, in no small way, determined by the suitability of the terrain. The Sennelager Training Centre has been a military prohibited zone under various political constellations since the nineteenth century and, as such, has been nothing else than the context for real war games; an area for combat training, violence and defence under controlled conditions; an experimental field for war and the "logistics of perception"[1].

C. Hils' pictures presented here are the result of many years of artistic-photographic field work in this area.

Although the material may be thematically and aesthetically homogenous, it is not organised as a series in which the individual photographs take up a specific position. To be sure, in the catalogue and exhibition, the observer is introduced to a certain series through the three broad thematic blocks – landscape, village and humanity. Yet, the order of the exhibition is not conceived as binding. Thus, as readers or observers, we are given the freedom to search for new connections and references both in and between the pictures. Along an optically thematic thread there gradually develops anew an inner logic of artistic documentation. The interpretation of the stories unfolds in the confrontation between the perspectives, views and spatial constructions in the photographs and the pictorial experience, associations and expectations of the observer.

Shooting pictures

The analogy of camera and weapon, drawn at the latest by E. J. Mareys in reference to so called Phase Photography, was extensively tested and researched both in a visual and technical respect as well as being verbally manifested. Recently, the inextricable connections to the shooting of photographs have been adequately analysed and methodically worked by P. Virilio and J. Baudrillard which, in no small way, is a result of the media experience of the war with Iraq. It is understandable that these pictures of the Senne provide the observer with this initial connotation. However legitimate and obvious as such an interpretation may be, the observer nevertheless ought not to avoid the effort of further exploring the pictures.

In the first instance, the camera perspective of the war games metaphor previously employed also reflects the artistic research in the style of photojournalism, hitherto inaccessible to the civilian public. To the untrained eye, its purpose is not recognisable. For a passerby, this area presents itself as a piece of nature leading its enclave existence without revealing itself; an apparent normality whose autocratic existence is almost invisibly staked out and guaranteed. It is only he or she who is willing to step across or break through these borders who will experience the implicit lie and the inversion of nature into calculation.

Just as this isolated and cut-off world does indeed reveal itself as a worldly model to the outside, conversely, so also may microcosmic states have an effect on our reality. In the pictures of the Senne, the experience of an apparent idyll of a contaminated environment is representatively visualised – as may be witnessed by the example of Chernobyl or by the causes of our daily experience of modern illnesses, invisible to our senses of sight and smell.

Erkundung eines für Zivilpersonen bisher unzugänglichen Geländes, das sich in seiner eigentlichen Zweckbestimmung dem Außenstehenden nicht zu erkennen gibt. Eine sich dem Vorbeifahrenden als ein Stück natürliche Natur präsentierende Gegend führt ein Enklavendasein, ohne sich preiszugeben; eine scheinbare Normalität, deren Autarkie und Eigenleben durch fast unsichtbare Zeichen abgesteckt und gewahrt wird. Nur wer diese Grenzen überschreiten oder durchbrechen will, erfährt den Trug des Sichtbaren und die Umkehrung des Natürlichen ins Kalkül.

Wie diese nach außen hin abgeschottete Welt sich innen sehr wohl als ein weltbezogenes Modell entpuppt, so lassen sich umgekehrt auch seine mikrokosmischen Zustände auf unsere Wirklichkeit unschwer beziehen. In den Bildern von der Senne wird stellvertretend die Erfahrung mit einer augenscheinlichen Idylle einer kontaminierten Umwelt visualisiert, wie wir sie am Beispiel von Tschernobyl oder anhand der unsichtbaren und geruchlosen „Erreger" unserer Zivilisationskrankheiten tagtäglich erfahren.

Ästhetik des teilnahmslosen Blickes

Nicht zuletzt stehen aber die Fotografien, der Inbegriff für die Abbildung der Realität, ebensosehr für die Skepsis und das Mißtrauen gegenüber der Offensichtlichkeit der Dinge überhaupt. Aus diesem scheinbar in sich widersprüchlichen Vorbehalt heraus formiert sich hier eine Ästhetik der Bilder, die mit dem Blick für das Nebensächliche und für das Unwirkliche dieser vermeintlichen Offensichtlichkeit der Faktizität entgegenzuwirken sucht. In den Bildern herrscht häufig eine merkwürdige Weitläufigkeit; wir bekommen völlig menschenleere Landschaften vorgeführt, die auch in der Komposition keine zentrale Motivik erkennen lassen. Die Topographie der Landschaft wird mit einer inhaltlichen Konnotation der Ereignis- und Bedeutungslosigkeit und

der Leere ins Bild transferiert. Auch dort, wo Spuren ins Blickfeld rücken, stehen sie nicht als „Gegenstand" des Bildes im Mittelpunkt. Sie füllen fast schon musterartig die gesamte Bildfläche und erwecken den Anschein des Selbstzwecks ästhetischer Formenspiele. Werden Panzer, Attrappen oder Figuren mit der Kamera eingefangen, so erscheinen diese scheinbar zufällig in der Ferne, am Horizont oder im Randbereich, der Aufmerksamkeit kaum würdig, so daß das Auge zunächst das Bildfeld absuchen muß, um sie in der Landschaft ausfindig zu machen. Es findet eine Dispergierung des Blickes statt, die von der vordergründigen Dokumentation des „Ist-Zustandes" abrückt und den Weg zu neuen Interpretationsmöglichkeiten öffnet. Hiermit wird ein Versuch unternommen, den vorgefundenen Fakten einen weiterführenden Sinngehalt abzugewinnen, indem gewohnheitsmäßige Sehweisen durch den gebotenen Rahmen des Kunstkontextes in ihrer Selbstverständlichkeit irritiert werden. Hieraus geht eine Bildsprache hervor, in der sich etwas mehr in der Abwesenheit als in seiner Präsenz zeigt: Die Dinge veranlassen uns durch ihren Hinweischarakter zu einer Spurensuche, die Fragen nach Erinnerung und Vergessen an einem Ort aufwirft, wo in historischer und geographischer Hinsicht eine einzigartige Verschachtelung von Geschichte sich sedimentiert.

Mit dieser Art der Bildfindung rückt C. Hils in die Nähe von jenen Künstlern, die, als Dokumentaristen der alltäglichen Banalitäten, sich eines Stils des scheinbar teilnahmslosen Blickes der Beiläufigkeit bedienen und den vorgefundenen Dingen dennoch eine überzeugende Symbolik abzugewinnen versuchen.[2] Ihr Zweifel an den Offensichtlichkeiten, aber auch an der Kraft der Bilder, rührt nicht zuletzt von den eindringlichen Bildeffekten der Medienwelt her, die uns gerade eine unhinterfragbare Glaubwürdigkeit und Authentizität suggerieren wollen. Die medienwirksame Aufbereitung von Politik, Ideologie und Gewalt überschüttet uns mit einer inflationären Bilderflut, die unsere Wahrnehmung

The aesthetics of the indifferent view

Finally, just as the pictures represent the epitome of the photographic reproduction of reality, they also represent scepticism and mistrust towards the clarity of things in general. Out of this apparent and in itself contradictory reservation an aesthetics of pictures emerges which, with a view to the secondary and unreal, attempts to counteract this apparent clarity of facticity. Frequently, a remarkable spaciousness predominates in the pictures; peopleless landscapes are presented to us that have no central significance for the composition. The topography of the landscape is transferred to the pictures with a connotation of its uneventfulness, meaninglessness and emptiness. Even there, where traces come into view, they do not occupy a central position as the 'object' of the picture. They fill the entire surface in an exemplary fashion and induce in the observer the impression of a game of aesthetic forms as an end in itself. Where tanks, dummies or figures are caught by the camera, they appear to be situated at a distance and as if by chance, on the horizon or on the periphery and with hardly any significance such that, at first, the eye is forced to select the field of vision in order to discover them in the landscape. A dispersal of the field of vision occurs which withdraws from the prominent documentation of the 'is-state' and which opens up the way to new possibilities of interpretation. An attempt is thus undertaken to extract a more far reaching significance from the facts, by means of which, within the framework of the artistic context, the habitual and self-evident ways of viewing things become irritated. A pictorial language emerges in which more is shown rather by the quality of absence than of presence: Through their indicative character, the things spur us on to search for traces that in one area throw up questions of remembering and of forgetting and where, from a historical and geographical perspective, a unique convolution of history is deposited.

With this method of discovering pictures, C. Hils comes close to those artists who cultivate, as documentarians of everyday banalities, a style of the apparently indifferent perspective and yet, at the same time, attempt to obtain from the things they document a convincing symbolism.[2] Their doubt about the obvious but also about the power of pictures, is in the end due to the insistence of the pictorial effect of the media suggestive, as it is, of unquestionable authenticity. The effective preparation of politics, ideology and violence swims over us in an inflationary flood of pictures which increasingly dim our senses. At this point the urgent question arises as to what other possibilities for artistic engagement remain. In view of the shocking pictures of the media today, art – to whose repertoire of avant-gardistic form also belong artistic provocation and shock – must search for a new means of creating pictorial meaning.

From a state of powerlessness and indignation, war photography frequently attempts to emotionalise and personify war in all its brutality, violence and pain so as to disconnect it from its distant and abstract appearance through the consternation and sympathy of the individual experience. With the increasing radicality of visual dissection, often the opposite of the above occurs: The closer the camera approaches the event, the more distant it appears to us. Sophie Ristelhueber formulates this hopeless form of witness with the following words: "After the process of description has come to a close, one discovers that nothing else is left. That is, where the process does create something, at the same time it destroys something else."[3]

Based on this experience, the pictorial aesthetics of the quieter and softer tones is the artistic attempt to intentionally work against the visual habits of this shuddering 'looking away' of the viewer. This stylistic

131

immer mehr abstumpfen läßt. Es stellt sich hierdurch die dringende Frage nach verbleibenden Möglichkeiten eines künstlerischen Engagements. In Anbetracht der Schockbilder der Medien muß heute die Kunst – zu deren avantgardistischem Formenrepertoire bisweilen gerade die künstlerische Provokation und der Schock gehörten – nach neuen Mitteln der bildnerischen Sinnstiftung suchen.

Kriegsfotografien sind häufig aus einer Ohnmacht und Empörung heraus bestrebt, den Krieg in seiner Aggressivität, Gewalt und den Schmerz zu emotionalisieren und zu personifizieren, um ihn durch die Betroffenheit und das Mitleid im Einzelfall von seiner entfernten und abstrakten Erscheinung zu entbinden. Mit der Steigerung der Radikalität visueller Sezierung widerfährt uns jedoch oft das Gegenteilige: je näher die Kamera an das Geschehen herangeht, um so entfernter erscheint es uns. Sophie Ristelhueber formuliert diese aussichtslose Zeugenschaft so: „Wenn der Vorgang der Beschreibung beendet ist, stellt man fest, das nichts mehr übrigbleibt. Das Verfahren erschafft zwar etwas, löscht aber gleichzeitig auch etwas aus."[3]

Die Bildästhetik der leisen Töne ist aus dieser Erfahrung heraus nicht zuletzt der künstlerische Versuch, dieser Sehgewohnheit des „schaudernden Hinwegschauens" engagiert entgegenzuwirken. Dieses Stilmittel kommt nicht selten in einer Bildpoesie zum Ausdruck, die angesichts der Thematik der Bilder auf den ersten Blick befremdend wirken mag und die sich nicht selten gegen den Vorwurf der Ästhetisierung und somit der Verharmlosung der Gewalt bzw. des Krieges wehren muß. „Schönheit (kann) ein sehr machtvolles Transportmittel für schwierige Ideen sein. Sie lädt die Menschen zu Dingen ein, bei denen sie normalerweise den Blick abwenden würden," argumentiert dagegen R. Misrach[4], deren metaphorische Wüstenfotografien ein „Spiegelbild für Militarismus, Gewalt und Zerstörung der Natur bieten"[5]. Ähnlich sieht auch der inzwischen

an Aids verstorbene Gonzalez-Torres, der mit seinen Bildern nicht zuletzt der Problematik seiner Krankheit Gehör verschaffen wollte, die politische Kraft der Ästhetik: „Manche Menschen behaupten, daß Ästhetik und Politik zwei verschiedene Dinge sind. Ich behaupte, daß der Aspekt der Ästhetik darin liegt, daß die Politik, von der sie durchdrungen ist, absolut unsichtbar ist. (...) In der Ästhetik geht es nicht um Politik – sie selbst ist Politik. Auf diese Weise kann das Politische am besten genutzt werden, da es so natürlich erscheint. Die erfolgreichsten politischen Handlungen sind jene, die nicht als politisch eingestuft werden."[6] Nimmt der Betrachter dieses Angebot der Hinführung zu schwierigen Themen durch die Bildästhetik an, wird er erfahren müssen, daß sich primär nicht die Radikalität, sondern der Wirkungsmechanismus des Schocks im Bild gewandelt hat. Der Schock in den Bildern C. Hils' setzt nicht durch die Provokation abschreckender Inhalte ein, auch nicht durch eine Ästhetik des Mitleides oder eines voyeuristischen Schauderns. Er setzt vielmehr durch die Kluft ein, die sich zwischen der Ästhetik der vordergründigen Normalität, ja Belanglosigkeit im Bild und dem sich dahinter verbergenden Sinngehalt auftut. Erst der Konflikt von Schönheit und Wirklichkeit, die Konfrontation einer durch die Ästhetik gespeisten Erwartung mit der eigentlichen Zweckbestimmung der Dinge, führt zu einer irritierenden Brechung der Kohärenz. Die Erfahrung, daß die künstlerische Rahmenverschiebung scheinbar konstante Offensichtlichkeiten zu fragwürdigen Variablen werden läßt, löst den Schock aus.

Wir lassen uns bei der Betrachtung des intensiv leuchtenden Gelb und des tiefen Blau der abstraktgesichtslosen Figuren von der expressiven Suggestivkraft der Matisseschen Farbpracht zu einem visuellen Genuß verleiten. Wir kosten die Spontaneität und Frische der großflächig aufgetragenen dicken Farbschichten vor dem schwarzen Hintergrund aus, denen durch partiell durchschimmernde schwarze Farbflecken eine eigenartige Textur verliehen wird. Unvermittelt

method, not uncommonly, comes to expression in the poetics of the picture. In view of the theme of these pictures, this may at first glance seem strange and which further may often lead to the accusation of the aestheticization of war and indeed, even that they play down violence and war. "Beauty (can be) an especially powerful medium for transporting problematic ideas. It invites people to consider things which, under normal circumstances, they would turn away from" argues R. Misrach[4], whose metaphoric photography of the desert "holds up a mirror against militarism, violence and the destruction of nature"[5]. Gonzales-Torres, a deceased AIDS victim who in his photography sought to establish greater public recognition of the problems surrounding his illness, saw the political power of aesthetics similarly: "Some people maintain that aesthetics and politics are two different things. I, however, maintain that aesthetics is permeated by politics which itself is invisible. (...) Aesthetics is not about politics, it is politics. It is in this form that the political can best be put to use because it appears so natural. The most successful political activities are those that have not been classified as political."[6] If the observer accepts this offer of guidance to these difficult themes through the aesthetics of pictures, he will experience that it is primarily not the radicality but rather the mechanism of shock that has changed in the picture. In the pictures of C. Hils, the element of shock engages neither through the provocation of the repulsive nor through the aesthetics of sympathy or voyeuristic pleasure in the horrific. Rather, Hils engages at the cleft between the aesthetics of the predominant normality, indeed, the triviality of the picture, and the concealed meaning. Only the conflict between beauty and reality – the conflict between expectation fed by aesthetics and the actual purpose of the objects – leads to an irritating break in coherence. The experience of an artistic shift of apparently self-evident constants to questionable variables gives rise to the shock.

We permit ourselves a visual pleasure by observing the intensely lit yellow and blue of abstract figures such as those of an expressive power of a Matisse. We taste the spontaneity and freshness of the thickly applied layers of colour in front of a black background which, through the partially glowing black flecks of colour, create an unique texture. However, this sense of pleasure is immediately shattered when we become aware that these anonymous figures emerge as targets and what was previously conceived of as a 'structural stylistic medium' – an invigorating surface structure of the forms – now appears to have emerged from the translucent impressions of rubber bullet holes having been painted over.

A surreal fascination begins with the fiery reds, 'blossoming' rusty flecks surrounding the bullet holes presenting themselves in the sun like a meadow strewn with field poppies. This idyll is erased only as one becomes aware of the series of events whose life-threatening traces have left their mark on the fixed target. Similarly, the mood, brought about by the composition of overlapping surfaces and layers, by clear air and the bright sun, is counteracted by the blurred appearance of a tank some distance away. The view through the small window towards this threatening piece of equipment draws the theme back into the picture.

From the interlocking of the aesthetics and atmosphere of nature and the metaphoric appearance of war, a picture-immanent conflict is initiated which, however, culminates in the shocked realisation of their incompatibility. This shock is set off by the unbearable experience that even in war, where madness reigns, normality, illusion and beauty still exist and by the anger that this remains outside of our reach as well as by the shame of taking advantage of this situation or even that we can derive aspects of beauty from these objects.

zerbröckelt jedoch dieses Wohlgefallen, sobald wir erfahren, daß diese anonymen Figuren als Zielscheiben fungieren und die zuvor als „gestalterische Stilmittel" rezipierte, belebende Oberflächenstruktur der Gestalten durch die durchscheinenden Abdrücke der in regelmäßigen Abständen übermalten Gummigeschosse entstand.

Eine surreale Faszination geht auch von den feuerroten, um die Einschußlöcher „blühenden" Rostflecken aus, die sich in der Sonne wie eine von Feldmohn übersäte prächtige Wiese präsentieren. Getilgt wird diese Idylle erst durch die Bewußtwerdung der Vorgänge, deren lebensbedrohende Spuren das abgestellte Festziel trägt. Ähnlich wird auch die durch die Komposition der einander überlappenden Flächen und Schichten, die klare Luft und die pralle Sonne verbreitete Stimmung konterkariert, sobald wir den in der Ferne verschwommen erscheinenden Panzer erblicken. Der Blick durch das kleine Fenster auf das bedrohliche Gerät bringt das eigentliche Thema ins Bild zurück.

Aus diesem Ineinandergreifen von einer Ästhetik der atmosphärischen Natur und der Optik der Kriegsmetaphorik bahnt sich ein bildimmanenter Konflikt an, der sich schließlich im Schock über diese Unvereinbarkeit entlädt. Ausgelöst wird dieser Schock durch die unerträgliche Erfahrung, daß selbst im Krieg, wo der Wahnsinn waltet, Normalität, Illusion und Schönheit existieren, in der Wut darüber, daß diese uns versagt bleiben und der Scham, wenn wir sie dennoch für Augenblicke in Anspruch nehmen oder mehr noch, wenn wir diesen Dingen unversehens Aspekte einer Schönheit abgewinnen können.

Die Kartographie des Krieges

Im engsten Sinne des Wortes können diese Fotos nicht als Kriegsfotografie bezeichnet werden. Zumindest dokumentieren sie nicht einen bestimmten Krieg, auf dessen Schauplatz wir uns befinden würden. Mit der Dokumentation von der Senne hat C. Hils vielmehr ein Thema gefunden, das auf eine sonderbare Weise zwei Schlüsselbegriffe der Kunst der 90er Jahre aufgreift und ihn in dieser Hinsicht in die Nähe der Land-Art Künstler rückt: Die Begriffe Dislocation und Displacement u.a. gehören zum Vokabular R. Smithsons, „um einen zeitgemäßen telematischen und postindustriellen Ortsbegriff zu entwickeln."[7] In diesem Zusammenspiel von fiktiven, konstruierten und realen Orten findet gewissermaßen eine Umkehrung von Virtualität und Realität statt, indem auf einem konkreten Ort andere konkrete Orte, die zuvor häufig auf telematischem Wege (z.B. Luftaufnahmen) erfaßt worden sind, realisiert werden. Zu Recht spricht Virilio von einer „synthetischen Vision", die eine unerläßliche Strategie moderner Kriegsführung darstellt. Aus der Synopse unterschiedlichster Bilder der Satellitenübertragung und deren digitaler Verarbeitung kann das Schlachtfeld in der Kommandozentrale jederzeit nach Belieben in einem vollständigen Panorama erfaßt und eine „Architektur aus Bildern" geschaffen werden.[8] Doch hier tut sich gleichzeitig auch ein Gegenpol zu Virilios Virtualisierungsthematik auf: Durch die provisorische Materialisation fremder Orte wird der konkrete geographische Standort aufgehoben und daher virtualisiert. Die reale Landschaft wird durch die Simulation fremder Kriegsschauplätze zum ideologisch territorial vereinnahmten Ort. Nicht die Immaterialisation und Auflösung, sondern die Konkretisierung und Konzentration, die Dichte des Ortes schafft das Unwirkliche. Auch Ubiquität, ein weiterer zentraler Begriff der telematischen Gesellschaft, kommt hier in einer ungewöhnlichen Deutung zum Vorschein. Nicht die Gleichzeitigkeit und Spaltung medialer Wahrnehmung des Menschen schafft die Möglichkeit, hier und dort zu sein, der Ort, der gleichermaßen hier

The cartography of war

In the strictest sense of the word, these photographs cannot be considered as war photography. At least, they do not document the scene of a specific war at which we could be present. With his documentation of the Senne, Hils has managed rather to identify a theme which in a peculiar way takes up two key art terms of the 90s and, in this sense, brings his work close to artists of Land-Art: The terms dislocation and displacement, among others, belong to the vocabulary of R. Smithson, "for the purposes of developing a contemporary telematic and post-industrial concept of location." This play between fictive, construed and real location represents a certain reversal of virtual and actual reality in which, in given concrete locations, other concrete locations that have been hitherto understood as telematic (e.g. aerial photographs) are realised. Virilio quite rightly speaks of a "synthetic vision", which represents an imperative strategy for modern warfare. On the basis of different pictures taken from satellite transmissions and digital processing, the battlefield can be comprehended in its entirety and at anytime by command and control centres and an "architecture of pictures" can be created.[8] Yet, at the same time, this opens up an antithesis to Virilio's theme of the virtual: Through a provisional materialisation of unfamiliar locations, a concrete geographical position can be dissolved and thereby be made virtual. The actual landscape thus becomes an ideological territory occupied by the simulation of an unfamiliar war scene. It is not immaterialisation and dissolution but concretisation and concentration – the closeness of the area – that creates the unreality. Ubiquity, another central term of the telematic society, appears here in an unusual interpretation. It is not the simultaneity and division of the medial perception of man that creates the possibility to be now here, now there; the location, which is

itself both here and there provides us with a personified omnipresence. The arbitrary manner in which this 'there' is employed and discarded depending on the political situation, the determination of the area as the point of crystallisation of war scenes, is the flip side of the coin of warfare. This manifold merging of space, location and projection is paradigmatically exhibited in the photo-series on the training village 'Tin City'. Like a colourful fictional matrix, the strategic marks of the planned game cover the doors and windows of the village houses. On the other hand, window curtains, advertisements, letter boxes and telephone boxes all signalise 'authenticity' between the corrugated iron fronts and stone houses of the streets. Video walls and watchtowers stand undeniably for invisible presence as well as omnipresent presentability.

At the Senne, we are presented with a cartographic impression of a war ideology which, according to Churchill, consists in the fact that, whereas in the wars of classical antiquity the various episodes of war were of much greater significance than the tendencies, in modern warfare, the tendencies have now become much more significant than the episodes.[9]

Similarly, for the photographer it is not war in the concrete, in its particular form of cruelty, that stands at the forefront of attention. Thus, the photographer's impersonal and humanly empty record offers no room for sympathy and empathy. With a war zone as a conglomeration of war as such, the photographer rather attempts to capture the tendencies and facts of war as a system which, according to its very nature, erases the individual and the singular and which, in the final analysis, is annihilation. This is demonstrated precisely by the fact that, in this location, both historically and geographically the most different segments of the world exist side

135

und dort ist, verschafft uns leibhafte Omnipräsenz. Die Willkür, mit der dieses „Dort" je nach politischer Situation herangeholt und wieder abgestoßen wird, die Bestimmung des Ortes als Kristallisationspunkt von Kriegsschauplätzen, ist die Kehrseite der medialen Kriegsführung. Dieses vielfache Ineinanderblenden von Raumerfassung, Ortung und Projektion wird in der Fotoserie über das Übungsdorf „Tin City" paradigmatisch vorgeführt. Wie eine bunte Matrix der Fiktion überziehen die strategischen Markierungen des Planspiels die Türen und Fenster der Häuser im Dorf. Vorhänge an den Fenstern, Werbeschilder, Briefkästen und Telefonzellen signalisieren hingegen „Echtheit" zwischen Wellblechfronten und Steinhäusern der Straßenzüge. Videowand und Wachposten stehen schließlich unmißverständlich für unsichtbare Präsenz wie für allgegenwärtige Präsentierbarkeit.

Wir bekommen in der Senne den kartographierten Abdruck einer Kriegsideologie vorgeführt, die nach Churchill darin besteht, daß im Krieg des Altertums die Episoden des Krieges von viel größerer Bedeutung waren als die Tendenzen; in der modernen Kriegsführung sind nun die Tendenzen viel bedeutender geworden als die Episoden.[9]

Auch für den Fotografen steht nicht der konkrete Krieg in seiner individuellen Ausprägung, in seiner konkreten Grausamkeit, im Mittelpunkt. Seine unpersönlichen und menschenleeren Aufnahmen bieten deshalb keinen Raum für Mitleid und Einfühlung. Mit einem Kriegsschauplatz als Sammelsurium des Krieges überhaupt versucht er vielmehr die Tendenzen, den Sachverhalt Krieg als System einzufangen, das seinem Wesen nach das Individuelle und das Einzelne tilgt und in seiner letzten Konsequenz die Vernichtung ist. Gerade die Tatsache, daß auf diesem einen Ort historisch und geographisch unterschiedlichste Segmente der Welt nebeneinander nachgebaut existieren, demonstriert diesen Sachverhalt. Das Nebeneinander der „Episode" – ob

Schauplätze in Korea, Irak oder Irland – schlägt in dieser willkürlichen Reihung politischer Zwischenfälle ins Beliebige um. Die Bilder analysieren den Krieg in seiner abstraktesten Form: in der fiktiven Einübung seiner Strategien für die konkrete Anwendung. Es wird eine Perspektive auf das Tendenzielle, Strategische und Rationelle eröffnet, in dem Menschen, wenn überhaupt, nur indirekt als anonyme Attrappen und Hindernisse, nur als Quantität existieren. Sachverhalte und Kategorien besitzen in diesem System je nach Zweckbestimmung nur temporäre Gültigkeit: Feinde und Verbündete, Täter und Opfer, Sieg und Niederlage oder Ursache und Wirkung sind nur Variablen und nicht Kategorien des Krieges. Die Waffen von heute sind die Attrappen von morgen.

### An der Nahtstelle von Technik und Natur

Dadurch, daß C. Hils das militärische Sperrgebiet, einen Ort höchster Zweckrationalität, nicht zuletzt als Landschaft, Gelände und Natur einfängt, vereint er in seinen Bildern zwei klassische künstlerische Konzepte des Bildraumes: die herkömmliche Toposdarstellung und die neuzeitlich-moderne Stimmungslandschaft. Der Schauplatz als Ort szenischer Handlung (hier des Krieges) und die Landschaft, ein Stimmungsraum, „der sich dem Betrachter in unmittelbarer Evidenz, (...) als rein ästhetische Erfahrung öffnet,"[10] werden in diesen Aufnahmen ineinandergeblendet. Nicht zuletzt läßt sich auch gerade in diesem Bildkonstrukt die weiter oben schon ausführlich beschriebene eigentümliche Ästhetik der Aufnahmen begründen. An dieser Demarkationslinie zweier Raumerfassungen werden auch die Grenzen und Möglichkeiten einer angemessenen künstlerischen Sprache des Bildes abgesteckt. Analogien zu diesem Bildkonstrukt finden wir neben der historischen Landschaftsmalerei durchaus auch in der Gegenwartsfotografie. Auf ähnliche Weise geht etwa A. Jaars in seinen Aufnahmen vor, wenn er Orte eines erst kurz zurückliegenden Massakers als augenscheinliche Idylle

by side in reconstructed form. The side-by-side existence of 'episodes' – whether the scene be in Korea, Iraq, or Northern Ireland – becomes in this arbitrary sequencing of political events itself arbitrary. The pictures analyse war in its most abstract of forms: In the fictitious exercise of strategy for the event of an actual war. A perspective on the tendential, strategic and rational is opened up in which human beings exist indirectly, if at all, as mere anonymous dummies and hindrances – as mere quantities. Depending on their purpose, in this system, facts and categories possess only temporary validity: Friend and foe, perpetrator and victim, victory and defeat or cause and effect are simply variables and not categories of war. The weapons of today thus become the dummies of tomorrow.

The link between technology and nature

In that Hils has captured the military prohibited zone – a location representing the highest form of functionality – as landscape, terrain and nature, he manages to combine two artistically classical concepts of pictorial space: Both the common topos representation and the modern atmospheric landscape. In these pictures, the scene, as the location of action (here, of war) and the landscape, an atmospheric space "which reveals itself to the observer as immediately evident, (...) as pure aesthetic experience"[10] are merged with one another. It is in this pictorial construction that the above described characteristic aesthetics of these pictures is grounded. The borders and possibilities of an appropriate artistic language of pictures can be delineated at this demarcation line of two different conceptions of space. Along with this historical landscape painting, we are able to find analogies to this picture construction in present day photography. A. Jaars has a similar approach as demonstrated in his pictures, whereby he captures the locations of recent massacres as an optical idyll of a tea field, a jungle street and a solitary cloud in a clear blue sky. Only in contrast to the hand written sketches below the pictures does the prominent appearance become broken and something of the inner compulsion of the statement and accompanying doubt about the possibilities of artistic representation first become visible.[11] In this twofold construction of the metaphorical landscape picture, in which he captures the scenes of the civil war in Northern Ireland, W. Doherty has also found a medium for visualising objects which "perhaps intellectually, politically or philosophically cannot be defined".[12]

Alongside research into the possibilities of artistic expression and the limits of the 'expressible', we witness in the works of Hils a new form of interpretation in this link between scene and landscape, which moves beyond the usual theme of war: War – understood as the culmination of technology ('the unchained beast') – is thematised in its violence towards nature. That is, in the broadest sense of the word, in Hils' pictures the dichotomy between nature and technology is articulated in language. Similar to the works of S. Ristelhueber, in Hils' work we are shown maltreated landscapes, "which have, above all, been deeply effected by the aggressive imposition of man."[13] Incidentally, where as S. Ristelhueber depicts the immediate destruction of military action, in his pictures, Hils also points to the parallels to our 'peaceful' treatment of nature in all its facets. The perverting of nature is also thematised, as demonstrated by the indulgent character of the golf course designed, as it is, for the recuperation of leading elites; the concrete paving over of the parade field or the hill used as a shooting range for small calibre arms which must be annually disposed of. The protective fire breaks destroy the earth no less than the destruction of the terrain used for tank exercises.

137

eines Teefeldes, einer Dschungelstraße und einer einsamen Wolke am blauen Himmel einfängt. Erst durch die Kontrastierung mit den handschriftlichen Skizzen unter den Bildern wird der vordergründige Anschein aufgebrochen und etwas von dem inneren Drang der Mitteilung und dem gleichzeitigen Zweifel an der künstlerischen „Darstellungsmöglichkeit" ansichtig.[11] Auch W. Doherty findet Mittel der Visualisierung von Dingen, die „sich vielleicht intellektuell oder politisch oder philosophisch gar nicht definieren"[12] lassen, in diesem doppelten Konstrukt des metaphorischen Landschaftsbildes, mit denen er Schauplätze des Bürgerkrieges in Nordirland festhält.

Neben der Erkundung künstlerischer Ausdrucksmöglichkeiten und der Grenzen des „Sagbaren" formiert sich aber bei C. Hils auch gerade an dieser Nahtstelle von Schauplatz und Landschaft im Bild ein neuer, über die gewohnte Kriegsthematik hinausführender Interpretationsstrang: Krieg wird – verstanden als die Kulmination der Technik („die entfesselte Bestie") – in seiner Aggression gegen die Natur thematisiert. Es wird also in den Bildern die Dichotomie von Natur und Technik im weitesten Sinne zur Sprache gebracht. Ähnlich wie bei S. Ristelhueber bekommen wir auch bei C. Hils geschundene Landschaften gezeigt, „die vor allen Dingen durch den Eingriff des Menschen tief getroffen wurden."[13] Während allerdings S. Ristelhueber die unmittelbaren Zerstörungen militärischer Handlungen vor Augen führt, zeigt C. Hils in seinen Bildern auch Parallelen zu unserem „friedlichen" alltäglichen Umgang mit der Natur in allen seinen Facetten auf. Thematisiert wird die Pervertierung der Natur, die sich für den Künstler in dem Hätscheln des Golfplatzes zur Erholung der Führungselite ebenso zeigt wie in der Pflasterung des Paradefeldes oder in dem Hügel der Kleinkaliberschießbahn, der jährlich als Sondermüll abgetragen werden muß. Die Brandschutzschneisen reißen den Boden nicht weniger aggressiv auf als die Schneisen des Panzerübungsgeländes. In einer

minimalistischen Formensprache, wie sie gerade diese Bilder innehaben, gelingt es C. Hils, die Nahtstelle dieser Dichotomie auch gestalterisch wirksam in den Aufnahmen einzusetzen.

Den gemeinsamen Nenner bei allen Formen der Nutzung bildet die Doktrin der Nützlichkeit, die selbst in einem ökologisch verantwortungsvollen Umgang mit der Umwelt irreversible Spuren hinterläßt. Unser Eingriff in die Natur richtet sich dieser Doktrin zufolge immer nur auf bestimmte Funktionen: Es wird ein beständiger Balanceakt zwischen Mobilisierung von Energien und Entwicklung von Absicherungsmaßnahmen geübt. Die künstlerische Repräsentation davon, daß dieses Naturverhältnis in allen Bereichen des von Menschen organisierten Ökosystems durchschlägt, bekommen wir in diesen Fotos überzeugend vorgeführt. Diese künstlerische Dokumentation erscheint als eine visualisierte Untermauerung einschlägiger Analysen unseres Bezuges zur Natur. Selbst unser Versuch, argumentiert etwa Gernot Böhme, die Selbstregulationsmechanismen der Natur wiederherzustellen, die Renaturalisierung der Bäche, das künstliche Anlegen von Feuchtgebieten oder die Rekultivierung ganzer Landschaften, die durch industrielle Nutzung verwüstet sind, „sind Formen von technischer Reproduktion von Natur"[14] und sind mit einem Funktionalismus behaftet. G. Böhme läßt uns in diesem Zusammenhang auch über die Beschaffenheit der ästhetischen Reproduktion der Natur, etwa in der Landschaftsplanung, keine Illusionen übrig. „Die Anerkennung, daß Naturschönheit ein Faktor von Lebensqualität ist, hat hier dazu geführt, daß sie zur planungsrelevanten Variablen geworden ist. Dabei gerät Schönheit ins Spannungsfeld konkurrierender Nutzungsinteressen um die knappe Ressource Natur."[15] Ähnlich wie G. Böhme, so scheint auch C. Hils die Unmöglichkeit und die Unfähigkeit eines anderen als technischen Naturverhältnisses des heutigen Menschen zu erkennen. Er macht uns in seinen Bildern die unwiderrufliche Zerstörung offenkundig, die wir durch unsere

In the minimalist language of forms which these pictures contain, Hils manages to effectively employ the link in this dichotomy.

The doctrine of utility forms the common denominator for all kinds of use which, even in an ecologically responsible treatment of the environment, leaves behind irreversible traces. Our intrusion into nature, according to this doctrine, always orientates itself on certain functions: A constant balancing act is exercised between the mobilisation of energy and the development of preventative measures. The artistic representation of the permeation of this relationship with nature into all areas of the ecosystem organised by mankind, is convincingly presented to us in these photographs. This artistic documentation appears as a visualised substantiation of relevant analyses of our relation to nature. Even our attempt, argues Gernot Böhme, to restore the self-regulating mechanisms of nature, the renaturation of streams, the artificial installation of marshlands or the re-cultivation of entire landscapes that have been ravaged by industrial use "are forms of technical reproduction of nature"[14] and are tied to a form of functionalism. In this connection, G. Böhme leaves us with no illusions as to the creation of aesthetic reproduction, for example, in landscape planning. "The recognition that natural beauty is a factor in the quality of life has, in this case, led to its becoming a relevant variable in planning. Beauty thereby falls into the conflict between competing functional interests for the limited resource nature."[15] Both Böhme and Hils agree that it seems impossible for contemporary human beings to have anything other than a technical relationship to nature. In his pictures, Hils makes abundantly clear the undeniable destruction we cause by our exploitative instrumentalisation of certain functions of nature. To be sure, the counteractive forces of nature's self-reproduction are also visible in the pictures. In these opposing tendencies of the technological and natural reproduction of nature, we sense something of the melancholy of an aesthetics of ruin in its simultaneously healing and painful transitoriness. The erosion and the overgrowing with new vegetation of old buildings, testing pools for tanks, reconstructed landing stages and trenches, however, not only imply the usual opposition of natural and human history. The visualisation of the forces with which nature demands the return of her areas is, at the same time, evidence that the human being's assault on the sphere of nature has left behind its irreversible impression.

The process of development appears to be unstoppable and it is this fact about which the pictures do not wish to, and cannot, deceive despite the prominence of an idyllic atmosphere. The fact that now the prohibited zone not only serves military purposes but also provides a multifarious field of activity for nature conservationists and historians offers only limited consolation. If one accepts Böhme's argumentation or if one consistently thinks through Hils' pictorial statements to the end, then the determination of the uses of the functionalistic approach to nature can hardly be seen as an opportunity for change. A positive prospect – as absurd as this may sound – appears to lie hidden rather more in the selective composition of functionality. Where we limit our functionality to certain fixed targets, we leave out other areas considered irrelevant in this connection. We cut out areas from our field of vision, we have 'blind spots' in our perception (of nature) so that, more or less unnoticed, uncontrolled events may develop within our environment. These come to the forefront through a renewed displacement of aims and acquire unexpected relevance in our functional framework. Thus, from the prohibited zone may emerge a nature reserve; from the bunkers of the Nazi period protected habitats for bats, and

139

ausbeuterische Instrumentalisierung bestimmter Funktionen der Natur verursachen. Zugleich werden gewiß auch die entgegenwirkenden Kräfte der Selbstreproduktion der Natur in den Bildern ansichtig. In dieser gegenläufigen Dynamik der technischen und der natürlichen Reproduktion der Natur spüren wir etwas von der Melancholie einer Ruinenästhetik in ihrer zugleich heilenden wie schmerzhaften Vergänglichkeit. Die Erosionen und Überwucherungen alter Bauteile, Panzerversuchsbecken, Landungsattrappen und Gruben durch eine neue Vegetation impliziert jedoch nicht nur die herkömmliche Gegenüberstellung von Erdgeschichte und Geschichte. Die Visualisierung der Kräfte, mit der die Natur ihre Bereiche zurückfordert, beweist auch zugleich, daß die Eingriffe des Menschen in die Natursphäre irreversible Spuren hinterlassen.

Der Prozeß der Entwicklung scheint unumkehrbar, darüber können und wollen die Bilder, trotz einer vordergründig idyllischen Atmosphäre, nicht hinwegtäuschen. Die Tatsache, daß das Sperrgebiet nun nicht nur militärischen Zwecken dient, sondern für Naturschützer und Historiker ein vielfältiges Betätigungsfeld darstellt, bietet nur bedingten Trost. Schließt man sich der Argumentation G. Böhmes an bzw. denkt man die Bildaussagen C. Hils' konsequent zu Ende, so kann in der Nutzungsbestimmung der Funktionalisierung von Natur kaum eine Chance der Veränderung gesehen werden. Eine positive Aussicht scheint vielmehr – so absurd es auch erscheinen mag – in der selektiven Beschaffenheit der Zweckrationalität verborgen zu sein. Während wir uns bedingt durch unsere Zweckrationalität auf ganz bestimmte Ziele fixieren, lassen wir andere, in dem gegebenen Zusammenhang irrelevante Sparten, außer acht. Wir blenden aus unserem Blickfeld Bereiche aus, haben „blinde Flecken" in unserer (Natur)wahrnehmung, so daß sich hierdurch, mehr oder weniger unbemerkt, unkontrollierte Vorgänge in unserer Umwelt herausbilden können. Diese gelangen erst durch eine erneute Verschiebung der Zielvorgaben zum Vorschein und

gewinnen unerwartet an Relevanz in unserem Funktionsraster. So können aus dem Sperrgebiet Naturschutzgebiet, aus dem Bunker der Nazizeit geschützter Lebensraum für Fledermäuse, aus der modernsten Waffentechnik Attrappen entstehen. – Und so können wir den Attrappen der Terroristenfiguren eine Ästhetik abgewinnen. Wie schmal allerdings der Pfad ist, auf dem wir uns hierbei bewegen, zeigt symbolisch der Balanceakt im Bild zwischen den Einschußspuren der Waffen und den Fußstapfen der Tiere. Als Sinnbild für die Überlappungen dieser Schichten von technischer Vereinnahmung und gezielt regenerativer Naturerhaltung kann jenes Bild stehen, dessen grüne Feldzonen scharf vibrierend durch ein rotes Band im Vordergrund und kaum wahrnehmbar durch einen Stacheldraht im Hintergrund durchtrennt sind. Das dunkelgrüne Laub hinter dem Zaun dient tatsächlich als Sichtschutz vor unbefugten Blicken – eine mechanische Absperrung und ein natürlicher Schutz für das Militärgelände – während das aggressiv in den Blick springende rote Band als Zugangsverweigerung zu der seltenen, inzwischen unter Naturschutz gestellten Vegetation dient, die sich absurderweise im Sperrgebiet von der Außenwelt verschont entfalten konnte.

Denkt man diese Schichtungen und Verschiebungen als Ausdruck eines sich wandelnden kulturell konstituierten Naturverständnisses, so kann es nicht weit hergeholt erscheinen, diesen Prozeß bis in den Bereich des Kunstkontextes zu denken. Durch die Transponierung der Naturverhältnisse ins Bild kann im übertragenen Sinne von einer weiteren, unsichtbaren „Absperrung", d.h. Distanzierung bzw. Positionierung des Menschen zur Umwelt gesprochen werden. Durch die Bildfläche bzw. durch den Rahmen des Bildausschnittes wird das Landschaftsbild selbst zum Ausdruck eines Naturverhältnisses des betrachtenden Subjekts. Natur wird zur Landschaft, die ihrerseits ein ästhetisch vermittelter Umgang mit der Natur und letzten Endes ein kultureller Entwurf ist. Insofern thematisieren die

derelicts from state-of-the-art weapons technology. In this way we can also obtain an aesthetics of dummy terrorist figures. How narrow the path on which we tread is can be seen symbolically in the balancing act depicted in one of the pictures between the traces of weapons shots and the imprints of animals. This picture could serve as a symbol for the overlapping of the various levels of technological demand and the targeted preservation of nature, whose sharply vibrating green field zones are divided by a red band in the foreground and, hardly discernible, by barbed wire in the background. The dark green foliage behind the fence, in fact, does serve as a visual screen for unauthorised eyes – a mechanical barrier and a natural protection for the military terrain; whereas the red band, aggressively jumping at the eye serves as a barrier to access the rare vegetation meanwhile placed under nature conservation which, absurdly enough, while protected from the outside world, has actually managed in the meantime to develop in the prohibited zone.

If one considers these layers and displacements as an expression of a changing, culturally constituted understanding of nature, it would not be too far fetched to think this process through to the sphere of the artistic context. Through the transposition of natural conditions into the picture, one can speak metaphorically of a further invisible barrier i.e. a distancing to or positioning of the human being within its environment. Through the surface of the picture or through the frame of the picture section, the picture of the landscape itself becomes an expression of the observing subject's relation to nature. Nature becomes a landscape which, in turn, is an aesthetically mediated approach to nature and which, finally, is a cultural design. In this way, the photographs thematise the conflict between nature and culture not merely in terms of their content:

They are themselves an expression of this condition. "Technically, nature becomes an instrument of human beings, whereas aesthetically, it becomes transfigured as landscape. In a symbolic exchange, disinterested contentment should compensate for practical subordination."[16] This has formed the critical foundation for the development of landscape painting since the 17th century. Photography, especially as a technical art can, in two senses, potentially include an alternating technical approach to nature: Art as the antithesis to technology but also to nature. To contemplate alternatives is not merely the preoccupation of romantics or, as a nature lover, urgently necessary. The disrespectful treatment of nature challenges us all the more – to quote Böhme once again – by means of our "newly won awareness, to talk of ourselves when referring to 'nature': The nature of which we are a part. The technical reproducibility of nature places our own self-understanding in question".[17] Thus, as humanly empty as Hils' pictures appear to be, the observer ought not to be blinded to the fact that, ultimately, they concern ourselves.

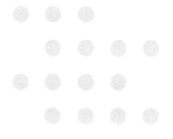

Fotografien den Konflikt zwischen Natur und Kultur nicht nur inhaltlich, sie sind selbst auch Ausdruck von diesem Verhältnis. „Technisch wird Natur zum Instrument des Menschen zugerüstet, während sie ästhetisch zur Landschaft verklärt wird. Interesseloses Wohlgefallen soll im symbolischen Tausch die praktische Unterwerfung abfinden."[16] So lautet die kritische Begründung zur Herausbildung der Landschaftsmalerei seit dem 17. Jahrhundert. Fotografie, insbesondere auch als technische Kunst, kann potentiell in zweierlei Hinsicht einen alternierenden technischen Umgang mit der Natur beinhalten: Kunst als Gegenpol zur Technik, aber auch zur Natur. Und über Alternativen nachzudenken ist nicht nur aus romantischen Überlegungen oder aus Naturfreundschaft heraus dringend notwendig. Der respektlose Umgang mit der Natur fordert uns erst recht heraus – um noch einmal G. Böhme zu zitieren – durch unser „wiedergewonnenes Bewußtsein, daß wir von uns selbst reden, wenn wir „Natur" sagen: von der Natur, die wir selbst sind. Die technische Reproduzierbarkeit von Natur stellt uns in unserem eigenen Selbstverständnis in Frage."[17] So menschenleer daher die Bilder von C. Hils auch sein mögen, so darf dies den Betrachter nicht darüber hinwegtäuschen, daß sie in erster Linie von uns selbst handeln.

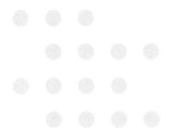

Epilog: Ein Stück Alltag

Mit diesen Tatsachen unausweichlich konfrontiert werden wir in den Bildern über die Schauplätze auf dem Nahkampfgelände. Zur Einübung des sekundenschnellen Ratespiels „Feind oder Nicht-Feind", „Schießen oder Schützen" wird dort eine merkwürdige Typologie des Zivilen entworfen. Ausgestattet mit den Ikonen des Alltäglichen erscheinen die Schaufensterfiguren – diese eigentlichen Söldner des Konsums – zum Artefakt „Durchschnittsbürger" entfremdet. Hastig eingekleidet verkörpern sie nun die umsorgte Mutter, den lässigen Freizeitmenschen, die mondäne Prostituierte oder den netten alten Herrn von nebenan. Diese eigenartige Ansammlung ausgesuchter „Normalitäten" führt uns nicht nur die erschreckende Banalität der vermeintlichen Erkennungsmerkmale des schutzbefohlenen „würdigen" Bürgers vor Augen. Unterschwellig dient es offensichtlich auch als Projektionsfläche einer vorenthaltenen Privatheit im Wehrdienst. Nur so läßt sich die akribische Sorgfalt erklären, mit der etwa die Preistafel des Fish-and-Chips-Verkäufers beschrieben oder das wirklichkeitsgetreu dekorierte Lokal mit einem ausgewählten Getränkesortiment an der Bar gestaltet sind. Diese plötzlich entdeckte Liebe zum eigentlich unwesentlichen Detail steigert nur den Kontrast zu jenen Signalen einer heimeligen Atmosphäre, die als obligatorisches Kruzifix über dem Sofa, als gemusterter Vorhang vor dem Wellblech oder als romantisches Altstadtbild an der Wand allein der Zielerkennung dienen. Daß die Figuren in dieser Inszenierung dennoch so deplaziert und bindungslos in Szene gesetzt erscheinen, macht es dem Betrachter bewußt, wie gezielt diese Typen jegliche Identität negieren und individuelle Lebensgeschichten tilgen.

Epilogue: A piece of everyday life

We are thus inescapably confronted with the facts depicted in these pictures of scenes in the close combat terrain. With the split-second guessing game of 'enemy or not enemy', 'shoot or protect' a remarkable typology of the civil has been drafted. Equipped with the icons of everyday life, the showcase mannequins – the real soldiers of consumerism – appear as alienated artefacts of the average 'citizen'. Hastily dressed, the mannequins now embody the caring mother, the individual at leisure, the mundane prostitute or the friendly old man from next door. This peculiar collection of selected 'normality' does not only present us with an appalling banality of assumed traits of the 'dignified' citizen who is to be protected. Subliminally, it clearly serves as a projection surface of a suppressed privacy during military service. Only in this way can one explain the meticulous attention to detail given to the price list of the fish and chip seller or the bar decorated, true to reality, with a selected assortment of drinks. This suddenly discovered love for unimportant detail only intensifies the contrast to those signs of a homely and familiar atmosphere such as the obligatory crucifix above the sofa, the patterned curtain in front of the corrugated iron or as a romantic old-town picture on the wall, which serve solely for target recognition. However, in that the figures of this production appear to be so displaced and so compliantly set in scene makes the observer conscious of how calculated these types negate all identity and erase individual biographies.

In the foreground, these pictures are concerned with a genre of normality which, however, express the perspective of a state of emergency. Behind the undefined absurdity of these photographs the same logic is concealed as that which influences our attitude to nature: Whatever values may form the basis of our actions, the measures for safeguarding the civilian population, as a form of re-cultivating the civilian in a state of war, they are military measures tied to the same functionalism as our re-naturation efforts with regard to the destruction of the environment. As natural beauty is limited in the face of the limited resource of nature, so also is the civilian in the face of the limited resource of peace a 'relevant variable among competing utilitarian interests'. We are given a symbol for the technical reproduction of peace by the mechanical devices upon which torsos are mounted and especially by the picture of the 'fleeing mother with child and assaulter on flip-up target'. The picture is dominated by an irritating contrarotation. Between the static of the composition and the explosive expression of the picture, there exists a picture-immanent rivalry which makes a satisfying interpretation almost impossible. Here, the compulsive suggestion to adjust the picture by 90° in order to dissolve the tension is almost unbearable. If we give way to this impulse it is almost as if we had pressed the trigger ourselves: The events rush up to us and we find ourselves to be at their centre.

Vordergründig geht es in diesen Bildern um eine genrehafte Normalität, die jedoch letztendlich die Perspektive des Ausnahmezustandes bekunden. Hinter der undefinierbaren Absurdität dieser Fotos verbirgt sich dieselbe Logik eines Zweckrationalismus, die auch unser Verhältnis zur Natur prägt: Welche Wertigkeit auch unseren Handlungen zugrunde liegen mag, die Absicherungsmaßnahmen der Zivilbevölkerung als Rekultivierung des Zivilen im Kriegszustand sind als militärische Maßnahme mit demselben Funktionalismus behaftet wie unsere Renaturalisierungsbemühungen in Anbetracht der Umweltzerstörung. Wie die Naturschönheit angesichts der knappen Ressource Natur, so wird auch das Zivile angesichts der knappen Ressource Frieden zur „planungsrelevanten Variablen unter konkurrierenden Nutzungsinteressen". Ein Sinnbild für die technische Reproduktion des Friedens liefern uns die auf mechanische Vorrichtungen montierten Torsi und insbesondere das Bild der fliehenden „Mutter mit Kind und Angreifer auf Klappscheibe". Das Bild wird von einer irritierenden Gegenläufigkeit beherrscht. Zwischen der Statik der Komposition und der explosiven Bildaussage besteht eine bildimmanente Rivalität, welche eine zufriedenstellende Interpretation beinahe unmöglich macht. Fast unerträglich wirkt hierbei die zwanghafte Suggestion, das Bild um 90° zurechtrücken zu müssen, um die Spannung zu lösen. Gibt man diesem Drang nach, so ist es, als hätte man auf den Auslöser gedrückt: Die Ereignisse rasen auf uns zu, wir befinden uns mittendrin.

ALFREDO JAAR, Field, Road, Cloud 1997
3 cibachrome prints mounted on plexiglas, framed
Color prints: 102 x 152 cm; B/W-prints: 15,5 x 23 cm

Courtesy Galerie Franck+Schulte, Berlin

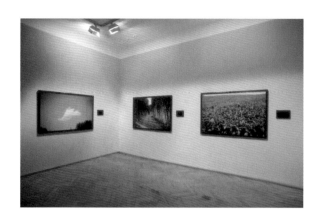

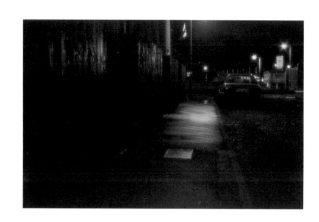

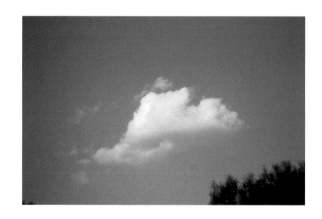

WILLIE DOHERTY, Out of the Shadows II

Courtesy Peter Kilchmann, Zürich

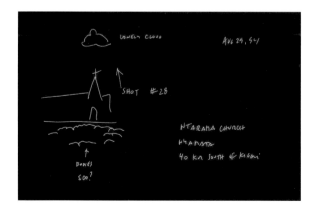

1 Vgl. den Buchtitel von P. Virilio:
Krieg und Kino. Logistik der Wahrnehmung,
Frankfurt a. M. 1989.

2 Zum Vergleich sollen hier einige Beispiele aus
dem Ausstellungskatalog der 3. Internationalen
Foto-Triennale Esslingen (1995) herangezogen
werden, die unter dem Motto „Dicht am Leben"
stand. So etwa die Arbeiten von Robert Adams
(1937), der in seinen Arbeiten über den
amerikanischen Westen und dessen Bedrohung
versucht, den Betrachter für die begrenzten
Ressourcen der Natur zu sensibilisieren.
William Eggleston (1939), der seine Motive aus
dem amerikanischen Alltag scheinbar wahllos,
im Stile der Schnappschußfotografie, aufnimmt.
„Leerstellen und ausgeschnittene Winkel
verleihen den Bildern eine geradezu provozierende
Beiläufigkeit." (Ausst. Kat. Esslingen, Hrsg. v.
R. Damsch-Wiehager, Ostfildern 1995, S. 128)
Er sagt über sich selbst: „Ich stehe auf dem Kriegs-
fuß mit dem Offensichtlichen" (ebd., S. 119).
Sophie Ristelhueber (1949), deren Fotografien
„eine indirekte Aussage über den Krieg [sind]
eine friedliche Betrachtung von Gewalt und
Verunstaltung, die uns daran erinnert, daß der
Krieg weder eine Wissenschaft noch eine Kunst
ist, sondern ein Zerstören und Zerquetschen
von Haut und Muskeln." (ebd., S. 137).

3 Ebd., S. 42.

4 R. Misrach: Violent Legacies.
Das Erbe der Gewalt. Drei Gesänge,
Frankfurt a. M. 1992, S. 90.

5 Ebd., Umschlag.

6 F. Gonzalez-Torres, in: P. Weibel (Hrsg.):
Inklusion: Exklusion, Graz 1996, S. 208.

7 P. Weibel (Hrsg.): Kontext Kunst,
Köln 1994, S. 48.

8 Ästhetik des Verschwindens. J. Nouvel
im Gespräch mit P. Goulek und P. Virilio.
In: ARCH+ Zeitschrift für Architektur
und Städtebau Nr. 108, S. 37.

9 Vgl. P. Virilio, S. Lotringer: Pure War. In:
Semiotext(e), Inc., New York 1983, dt.:
Der reine Krieg, Berlin 1984, S. 17.

10 B. Wyss: Vom Schauplatz zur Landschaft. In:
K. Becker, K. Wallner (Hrsg.):
Landschaft. Mit dem Blick der 90er,
Köln 1995, S. 12.

11 Fotografie als Handlung – Photography as
Concept. 4. Internationale Foto-Triennale
Esslingen 1998, Ostfildern 1998, S. 92–95.

12 Ebd., S. 76f.

13 R. Damsch-Wiehager (Hrsg.):
3. Internationale Foto-Triennale Esslingen 1995,
Ostfildern 1995, S. 137.

14 G. Böhme: Natürlich Natur. Über Natur im
Zeitalter ihrer technischen Reproduzierbarkeit.
Frankfurt a. M. 1992, S. 112.

15 Ders.: Für eine ökologische Naturästhetik.
Frankfurt a. M. 1989, S. 26.

16 B. Wyss, 1995, S. 20.

17 G. Böhme, 1992, S. 109.

1 cf. the title: Krieg und Kino. Logistik der Wahrnehmung, Frankfurt a. M. 1989

2 for a comparison a number of examples may be drawn from the exhibition catalogue of the 3rd Internationale Photo-Triennale, Esslingen (1995) under the motto title "Dicht am Leben". So, for example in the works of Robert Adams (1937) who, in his works on the American West and the threat it was under, sought to sensitise the observer to the limits of natural resources. William Eggleston (1939), who apparently took his motives from everyday life in America arbitrarily in a random snapshot photographic style. "Empty places and cut out corners provide the pictures with a casual tone". (Ex. cat. Esslingen published by R. Damsch-Wiehager, Ostfildern 1995, p. 128). He said of himself: "I stand at loggerheads with the obvious" (ibid p.119). Sophie Ristelhueber (1949), whose photographs are "an indirect statement on war and a peaceful reflection on violence and disfigurement and which reminds us that war is neither a science nor an art but rather a destruction and a crushing of skin and muscle". (ibid, p.137)

3 ibid, p. 42

4 R. Misrach: Violent Legacies. Das Erbe der Gewalt. Drei Gesänge, Frankfurt a. M. 1992, p.90

5 ibid, cover

6 F. Gonzalez-Torres, in: P. Weibel (ed.): Inclusion: Exclusion, Graz 1996, p.208

7 P. Weibel (ed.): Kontext Kunst, Cologne 1994, p. 48

8 Ästhetik des Verschwindens. J. Nouvel im Gespräch mit P. Goulek und P. Virilio. In: ARCH+ Zeitschrift für Architektur und Städtebau Nr. 108, p. 37

9 cf. P. Virilio, S. Lotrienger: Pure War, in: Semiotext(e), Inc., N.Y. 1983

10 B. Wyss: Vom Schauplatz zur Landschaft, in: K. Becker, K. Walner (ed.): Landschaft. Mit dem Blick der 90er, Cologne 1995, p.12

11 Photographie als Handlung – Photography as Concept, 4. Internationale Photo-Triennale Esslingen 1998, Ostfildern 1998, pp. 92-95

12 ibid, p.76 f.

13 R. Damsch-Wiehager (ed): 3. Internationale Photo-Triennale Esslingen 1995, Ostfildern 1995, p.137

14 G. Böhme: Natürlich Natur. Über Natur im Zeitalter ihrer technischen Reproduzierbarkeit, Frankfurt a. M. 1992, p.112

15 G. Böhme: Für eine ökologische Naturästhetik, Frankfurt a. M. 1989, p.26

16 B. Wyss, 1995, p.20

17 G. Böhme, 1992, p.109

Zielobjekt für Gummigeschosse: Terrorist 1 | Target for rubber bullet: Terrorist 1

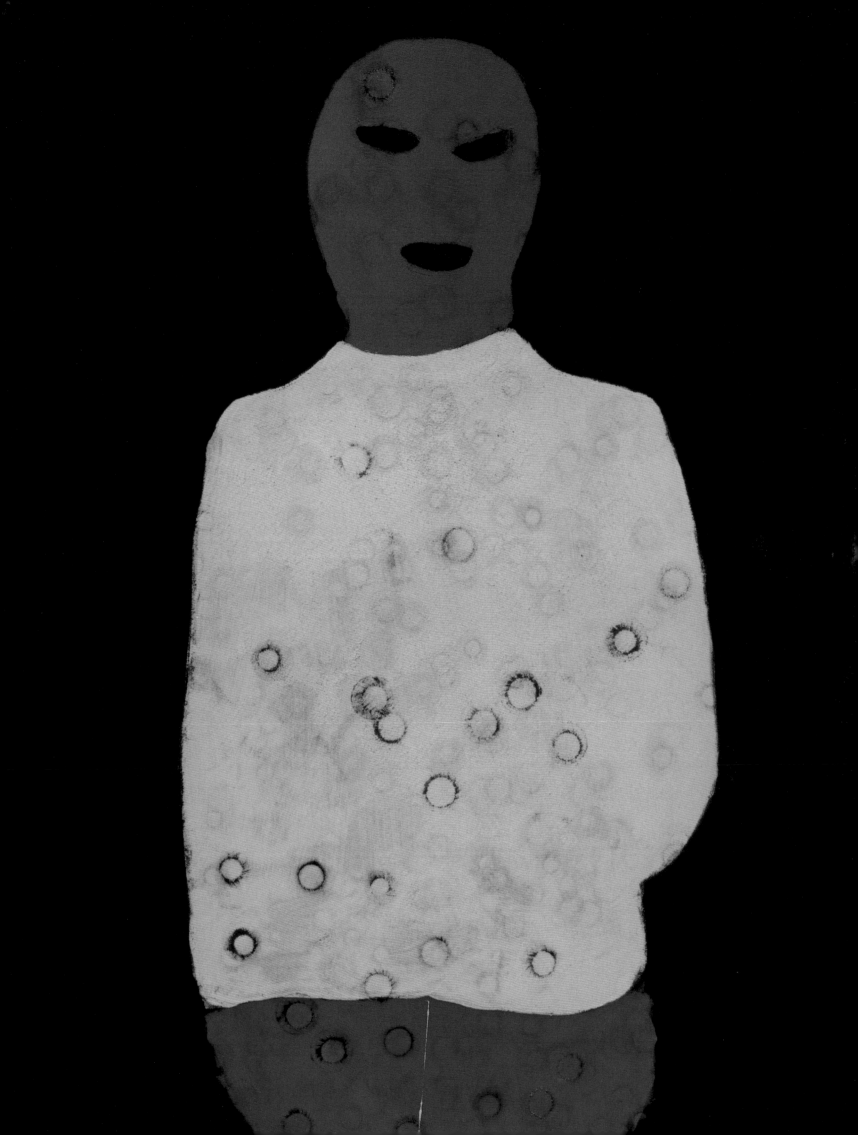

Zielobjekt für Gummigeschosse: Terrorist 2 | Target for rubber bullet: Terrorist 2

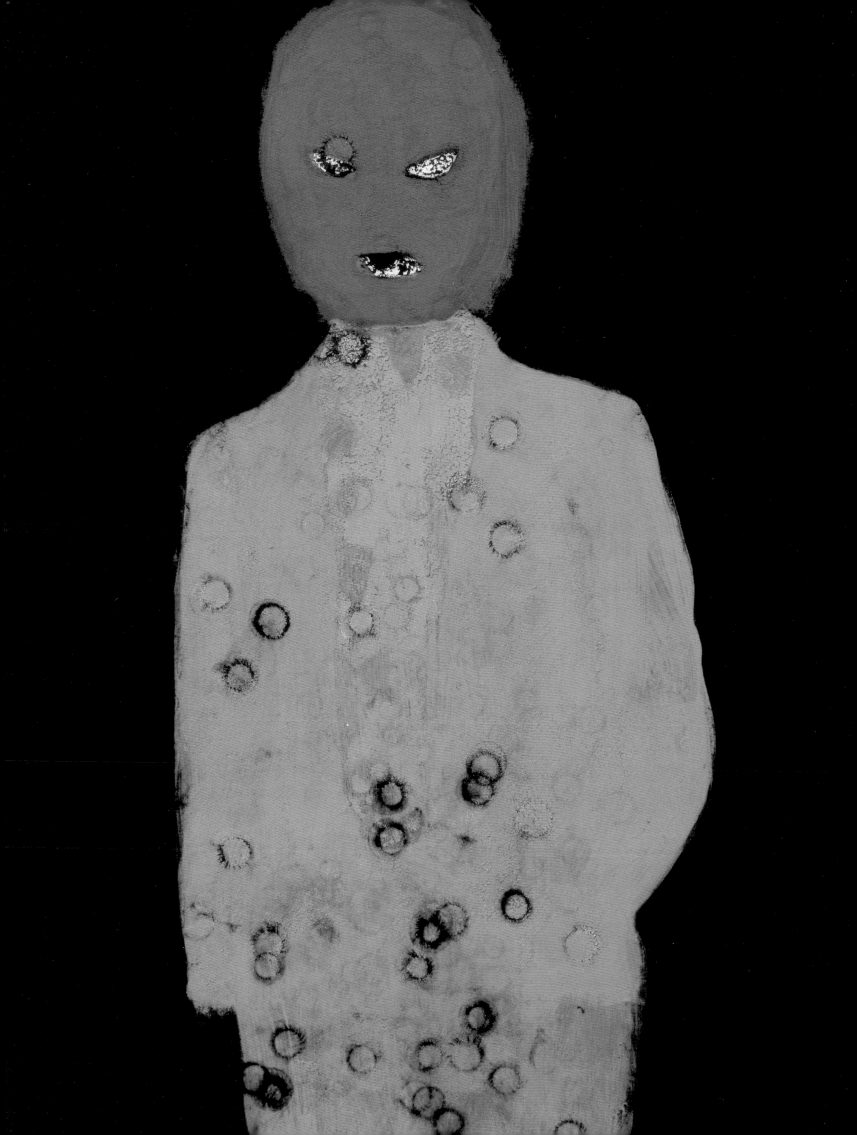

Zielobjekt für Gummigeschosse: Terrorist 3 | Target for rubber bullet: Terrorist 3

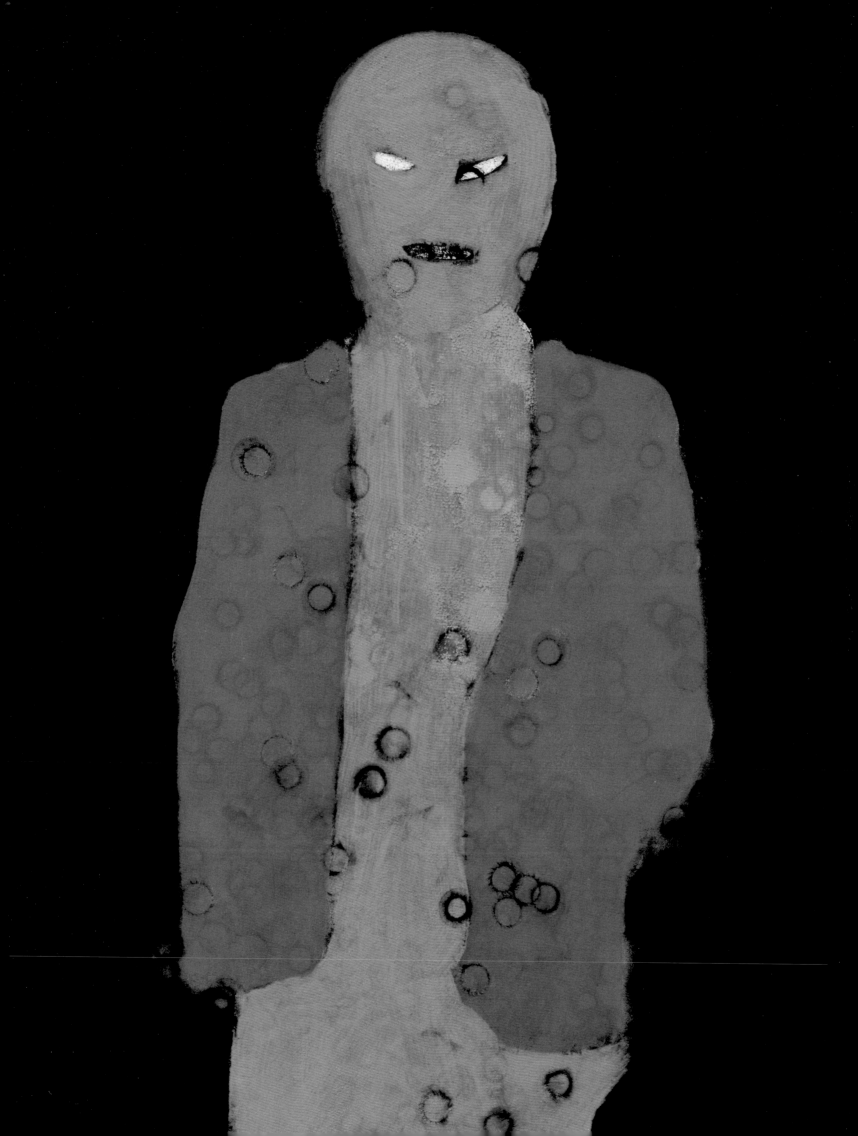

Biographien

Fotograf                Claudio Hils

                        Geboren 1962 in Mengen, Baden-Württemberg.

                        Studium der visuellen Kommunikation an der
                        Universität GH Essen.

                        Arbeitsgebiete: Journalismus und Fotografie, Konzeption und
                        Gestaltung von Ausstellungen und Printmedien.
                        Buchpublikationen.

                        Er lebt und arbeitet in Essen.

Autoren                 Anna M. Eifert-Körnig

                        Geboren 1956 in Ungarn.

                        Studium der Kunstgeschichte, Philosophie und Ethnologie in
                        Tübingen und Basel; Dr. phil.; Lehrtätigkeit an den Universitäten
                        in Tübingen, Dresden und Stuttgart.

                        Veröffentlichungen zur Gegenwartsarchitektur, Fotogeschichte
                        und Medienkunst.

                        Sie lebt in Darmstadt.

                        Rolf Schönlau

                        Geboren 1950 in Paderborn.

                        Studium der Literaturwissenschaft und Psychologie
                        in Berlin und München.

                        Er lebt und arbeitet als freier Autor in Schlangen, NRW.

Biographies

Photographer          Claudio Hils

Born 1962 in Mengen, Germany.

Studied Visual Communication at
Essen University, GH Essen.

Fields of work: Journalism and Photography. Conception and
Design of Exhibitions and Printed Media. Book Publication.

He lives and works in Essen.


Authors          Anna M. Eifert-Körnig

Born 1956 in Hungary.

Studied Art History, Philosophy and Ethnology at the
universities of Tübingen, and Basel; PhD; teaches
at the universities of Tübingen, Dresden and Stuttgart.

Publications on the themes of contemporary architecture,
history of photography and media art.

She lives in Darmstadt.


Rolf Schönlau

Born 1950 in Paderborn, Germany.

Studied Literature and Psychology
in Berlin and Munich.

He lives and works as a free-lance author
in Schlangen, North Rhine-Westphalia.

Danksagungen | Acknowledgements

Red Land – Blue Land ist das Ergebnis einer langjährigen, engen Zusammenarbeit zwischen dem Bildautor Claudio Hils und dem Textautor Rolf Schönlau.

Ausstellung und Katalog wurden gefördert vom Ministerium für Arbeit, Soziales und Stadtentwicklung, Kultur und Sport des Landes Nordrhein-Westfalen, dem Kultursekretariat NRW Gütersloh, dem Landesverband Lippe, dem Lippischen Heimatbund und dem Color-studio 27, Essen.

Besonders bedanken für die freundliche Zusammenarbeit und engagierte Unterstützung möchten sich die Autoren bei Ernst Abrahams, Marina Albrecht, Manfred Böcker, Oliver Bottenbruch, Patrick Butterly, Gerhard Hegemann, Gerd Helfferich, Wolfgang Herbig, Hellmut Holländer, Theo Immisch, Joachim Irmler, Meinolf Jansing, Vera Lüpkes, Justin Morris, Ralf Noske, Nicole Richardson, Ernst-August Schepmann, Manfred Schmalriede, T. K. Schütte, Walter Stich, Axel Stoffers, John Thompson, Christa Vennegerts, Georges Vercheval und Martin Waters.

Red Land – Blue Land is the culmination of many years of co-operation between photographer, Claudio Hils and author, Rolf Schönlau.

The exhibitions were sponsored by the Ministry of Employment, Social and Urban Development, Culture and Sport of the state of North-Rhine Westphalia, the Secretary for Culture NRW, Gütersloh, the State Council, Lippe, the Lippe Local Association and Colorstudio 27, Essen.

The authors and photographer would like to express their warm thanks for the friendly co-operation and enthusiastic support of the following persons: Ernst Abrahams, Marina Albrecht, Manfred Böcker, Oliver Bottenbruch, Patrick Butterly, Gerhard Hegemann, Gerd Helfferich, Wolfgang Herbig, Hellmut Holländer, Theo Immisch, Joachim Irmler, Meinolf Jansing, Vera Lüpkes, Justin Morris, Ralf Noske, Nicole Richardson, Ernst-August Schepmann, Manfred Schmalriede, T. K. Schütte, Walter Stich, Axel Stoffers, John Thompson, Christa Vennegerts, Georges Vercheval, and Martin Waters.

Ministerium für **Arbeit,**
**Soziales** und **Stadtentwicklung,**
**Kultur** und **Sport**
des Landes
Nordrhein-Westfalen

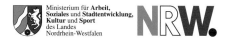

**NRW.**

---

*Orangerie Schloß Brake*

INSTITUT FÜR
LIPPISCHE
LANDESKUNDE

---

Kultursekretariat
NRWGütersloh

---

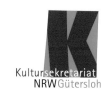

LIPPISCHER HEIMATBUND

---

ColorStudio 27  Müller und Pung GmbH
Visualisierungen

---

Karte des Truppenübungsplatzes Senne
(nicht maßstabsgetreu)

Map of Sennelager Training Area
(not true to scale)

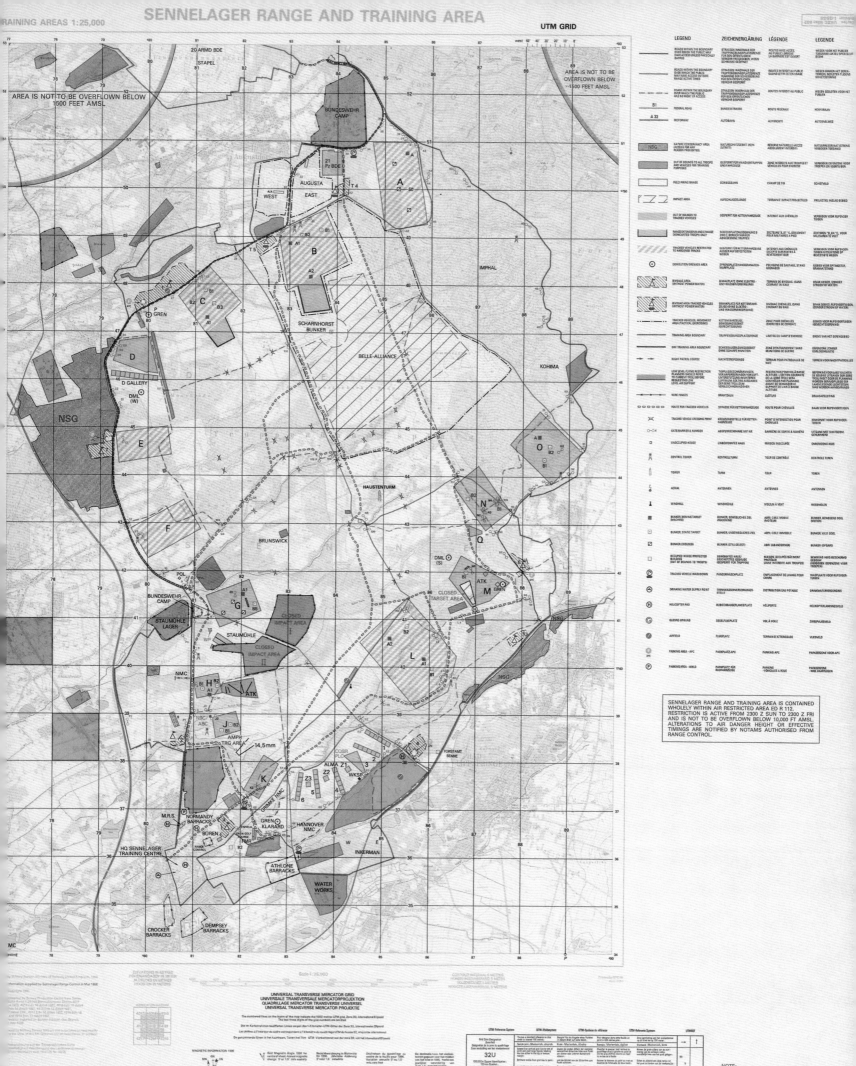

Impressum | Colophon

Erschienen im | Published by
Hatje Cantz Verlag
Senefelderstraße 12
D-73760 Ostfildern-Ruit
Tel. ++ 49-7 11-4 40 50
Fax  ++ 49-7 11-4 40 52 20
Internet: www.hatjecantz.de

Distribution in the US
D.A.P., Distributed Art Publishers, Inc.
155 Avenue of the Americas, Second Floor
USA-New York, N.Y. 10013-1507
Tel. 0 01/2 12/6 27 19 99
Fax 0 01/2 12/6 27 94 84

ISBN 3-7757-0930-4

Printed in Germany

| | |
|---|---|
| Konzeption \| Conception | Claudio Hils |
| Lektorat \| Editing | Nicole Richardson, Anja Schrade |
| Übersetzungen \| Translations | Justin Morris, Patrick Butterly |
| Gestaltung \| Graphic Design | gruppeDREI, Essen |
| Vergrößerungen \| Prints | Axel Stoffers, Claudio Hils |
| Reproduktion \| Reproduction | Kaufmann Prepress, Stuttgart |
| Gesamtherstellung \|Printed by | Dr. Cantz'sche Druckerei, Ostfildern-Ruit |